Welcome

 Stretch your Windows XP muscles! This handy reference guide is all you need to really unleash the power of your operating system

Think you've explored all there is to explore? Tried all you can try? Mastered Windows XP fully and completely? Think again. This book will change your mind.

We've trawled the pages of *Windows XP: The Official Magazine* to bring you the most advanced bits together, under one roof.

From advanced memory techniques, to ways to maintain your system more effectively, we have it all.

We show you ways to configure your system to make more efficient use of resources, clever tweaks you can make to the Registry, and some massive improvements to the way you can use Windows Messenger.

Finally, we've grabbed together 50 ways you can boost the speed of your Windows XP system. You may think it's fast enough, but if like us you want the absolute maximum performance your PC is capable of delivering, these tips are exactly what you'll be looking for.

We hope you enjoy this, the third in our recent series of collectable tips book. Any comments, ideas and suggestions are always welcome – just email me. ■

David Bradley,
Editor

Email: david.bradley@futurenet.co.uk

Contents

7. Windows Messenger

8. ABC of upgrading

9. Go further with Windows XP

10. 50 speed tips

Making the most of memory

14 Optimising and checking memory

How to check your memory allocations and tweak them to get the fastest performance from your PC

18 Monitoring your virtual memory

What is virtual memory and how can you use it to make your PC more efficient? Find out here

21 Our pick of the top memory tools

Five top utilities to optimise your memory use – download them for free now!

Make more of memory in Windows XP

Memory has a huge impact on your PC's performance: make sure it's doing the best it can with our full guide

For those used to juggling memory in Windows 95, working with Windows XP is a refreshing change as there's no arbitrary limit on system resources. As long as you've got enough memory free (or enough empty space on your hard drive to use as virtual memory), your computer won't slow down just because it needs to store more than 64K of information about the different programs that are running.

Windows XP manages memory better as well: it doesn't let drivers insist on getting memory when there isn't enough to go round, it takes memory back from programs that aren't using as much as they asked for, it can keep track of around 1GB of memory so it knows exactly which information needs to be in real, fast memory and which can go in slow, virtual memory and if you're running so many programs that you're almost out of memory, it slows everything down so it can keep working safely.

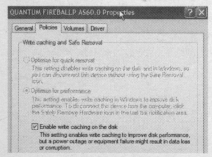

Make sure your hard drive is transferring information as efficiently as possible

Changing the registry settings isn't hard, but keep a note of what you change in case you need to change it back

Buy big

Even though Windows XP does a good job of managing your memory, there are a few things that you can do to help. For a start, buy as much memory as you can afford – more real memory will make a big difference to the performance of your system and memory is still fairly cheap. Windows XP will run in 64MB of RAM but you won't get the most out of it because so much of what you're working on will have to be saved to disk instead.

This is called paging because the system loads a 'page' of information into memory at once (or saves a 'page of information' from memory to the hard drive). While 128MB or 256MB is better, if you can afford it try to get at least 512MB of RAM in your PC: it will feel like a whole new PC and can cost as little as £60.

≫ Optimise memory with TweakXP

If you don't fancy editing the Registry and running performance tests to see what are the best settings for your system, try a utility like TweakXP. It collects together a comprehensive list of standard system settings with obscure Registry hacks in a friendly interface.

You can use the RAM optimiser to reorganise memory before you launch a program that needs a lot of memory. You can also do a lot of the work of tweaking your page file and the Registry settings for memory management with the cache optimisation tool, allocating more memory for I/O caching to improve the performance of your disk or optimising memory to speed up applications.

You can also force Windows to keep the kernel in memory (if you've got at least 512MB RAM), which will speed up most programs: if you run several large applications at once this can actually slow your system down because the kernel takes up the RAM the programs would otherwise have used, so it's handy to be able to turn it off easily if it's not helping.

Change Registry settings without having to edit the Registry by hand using TweakXP

Update drivers

Next, check your drivers and applications: are they up to date? New releases of drivers and updates to programs often fix memory leaks. Signed drivers have passed a full set of tests so they should be efficient.

If you don't know exactly how much memory something is using, launch the Task Manager (Ctrl-Alt-Del) while you're using it and look at the page file usage (the page file is the file on your hard drive that Windows uses as virtual memory, sometimes called swap space or the swap file). That tells you how often Windows needs to use virtual memory while you're using that application.

Check memory usage

Run the System Monitor (in the Performance tool on the Administrative tools menu). Click the Add button on the toolbar and choose Process; pick the application you want to check and choose Working set from the list of counters – that's how much memory it's using at any one time.

You can see the minimum and maximum working set for the program in the System Information tool (Accessories, System Tools on the Start menu). Then close the application and look back at the page file in Task Manager to see how much less is in use. If you can add that much real memory, you'll speed up the application dramatically.

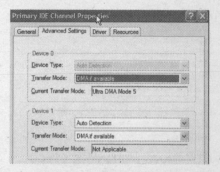

If you can't add any more memory, make the most of what you've got installed. It's worth making sure that the hardware in your PC is set up as efficiently as it can be and there are a number of memory management settings it's worth checking.

Change Page File settings

You can also change the page file itself. You'll need to spend some time looking at how your memory is being used but then you can change where the page file is stored and how large it is or defragment it if necessary. If you've got two different hard drives you can improve performance by putting the page file on the one you use less or splitting it across two disks. If you've only got one drive, fixing the size of the page file can boost your performance because Windows

Unless you've got lots of memory or you're running a server, concentrate memory on applications, not the system cache

doesn't waste time making the file larger and smaller as you open and close applications. But before you start any of these tweaks, always make sure that you've got a backup of your files and use System Restore to save your settings in case anything goes wrong.

Open System Restore from the Performance and Maintenance control panel and select Create a restore point before each and every major change you make.

Get more from your chips

Although the memory chips inside your PC and the hard drive that makes your virtual memory are physical hardware that you can't alter, you can change the way your PC deals with them, and that can improve the performance of your whole system. Although the speed of the processor and the capabilities of the screen and graphics card affect how fast your PC can work things out and how fast it can show them to you, what really affects performance is how much memory you have and how fast it is.

Restart your PC, and before Windows boots up you'll see a message on screen telling you how to get into your BIOS configuration. Look in the Advanced section for DRAM timing settings: these control how fast the PC expects the memory to be. Look for a setting called Auto (SDRAM configured by SPD on PCs with Asus motherboards) to

have the motherboard interrogate the Serial Presence Detect – a ROM on the memory chips that stores the parameters of the memory, which gives you the best timings with the least fuss.

Alternatively, look in your PC manual or get the chip numbers from your RAM and look them up on a memory site like www.crucial.com to find the fastest speed.

Speed up your hard drive

Next, make sure your hard drives are configured to transfer data as fast as possible. Open the Device manager (from the Hardware tab of the System Properties control panel) and open the list of disk drives. Right-click on your hard drive and choose Properties, Policies and make sure that Enable write caching on the disk is ticked. If you have a SCSI hard drive you'll see a SCSI Properties tab with extra settings: unless you're having problems with your hard drive, make sure that Disable Tagged Queuing and Disable Synchronous Transfers aren't ticked as they slow down the transfer of I/O commands and data packets to the disk.

Now open the IDE ATA/ATAPI controllers tree and for both the Primary and Secondary IDE Channel choose Properties, Advanced Settings. You should make sure that the Transfer Mode is set to DMA if available for all the channels. Direct Memory Access enables your PC to transfer data between memory and the hard drive without going via the processor. That gives you faster data transfer and leaves the processor free to get on with running your software.

Tweak the Memory

Once your hardware is running as fast as it can, look at how memory management is configured. On the Advanced tab of the System Properties control panel tick Performance Settings, Advanced.

In some cases, Windows XP configures your PC to be good at sharing files and devotes a lot of memory to the file system cache so that the Windows kernel runs in real memory and none of it is pages to disk.

If you have enough memory for your applications to run as well this can speed your system up. If you haven't, your applications end up using virtual memory and your system spends a lot of time swapping between real memory and virtual memory. You can turn the system caching off simply by changing the Memory usage setting to Programs.

Tweak the Registry
You can change the Registry settings by editing them directly (choose Start, Run and type in Regedit to open the Registry Editor) or via tweaking utilities like TweakXP. In the Registry Editor go to the [HKEY_LOCAL_MACHINE\SYSTEM\CurrentControlSet\Control\SessionManager\Memory Management] key.

Not all of the sub-keys here will improve performance: ClearPageFileAt Shutdown wipes the page file when you turn off your PC, but that's more for security and leaving it disabled gives you a faster shutdown. LargeSystemCache is the same as the Memory usage option in System Properties. If you have a lot of RAM, experiment with turning off virtual memory altogether by setting DisablePaging Executive to 1.

If there is an entry for IOPage LockLimit this limits the memory that Windows can reserve for doing file transfers – unless you do a lot of file copying and sharing you don't really need this setting.

The default value is 512K (in bytes) but

System shortcuts

■ You'll be working a lot with the System Properties control panel which you can open rapidly by holding down the Windows key and pressing the Pause/Break key. If you want to get at all the different control panels quickly, right-click on the Start button and choose Properties, Start menu, Customise, Advanced and change Control Panel to Display as a menu.

increasing it to between 8 and 16MB can improve performance. The PagingFiles key stores the location of the page file and the initial and maximum sizes.

STEP BY STEP

>> Checking memory usage

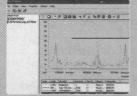

1 TASK MANAGER Use this to see how much real and virtual memory is in use and how much information is being paged to disk.

2 SYSTEM INFORMATION Use the System Information tool to see the minimum and maximum memory that your applications ask for.

3 SYSTEM MONITOR Use the System Monitor to see how much memory an application actually uses (the thick black line on the graph).

Virtual Memory

You can control how your PC uses virtual memory to speed up your PC's performance, using the built-in tools. Here's how

Unless you have an enormous amount of RAM in your PC, you never have enough real memory to run all the applications you want so your PC uses the hard drive to make up the shortfall. Windows XP is very good at managing the space it uses on your hard drive but because every PC is different you can make it more efficient by tweaking the settings.

Everything you do with your computer happens in memory, until you save a file to disk. To give programs more memory, Windows XP reserves an area of the hard drive, called the page file. When a program needs information that's in virtual memory, Windows XP swaps a chunk of information that's currently in memory but not being used for the chunk of information the

program wants to use; these chunks are called 'pages' of memory.

The page file is called PAGEFILE.SYS and you'll find it in the root of your C: drive if you've told Explorer to show you hidden system files (choose Tools, Folder Options, View and first select Show Hidden Files and Folders then clear Hide Protected Operating System Files). You can't change the page file directly; instead you change virtual memory settings in the System Properties control panel to alter how large the page file is and where it's stored.

With two different hard drives in your PC, you can speed up your system by putting the page file on the one you use less (as long as it's not a slower disk) or splitting it across both disks. With only one hard drive you can

---

>> Monitoring Windows XP memory

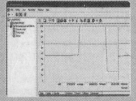

1 **SEE IT IN SYSTEM MONITOR**
Watch memory while you're working with System Monitor in the Performance console (under Administrative tools on the Performance and Maintenance Control Panel); click the Add button to add counters.

2 **LOG COUNTERS**
Track memory and the page file over a longer period of time with a log file. Pick Counter Logs under Performance Logs & Alerts, right-click in the main window and choose New log settings then Add the counters to track. Click Close to start.

3 **SEE THE LOG**
Windows XP puts the log files in C:\PerfLogs; open your log file in Notepad or Excel. If you're tracking page file usage the percentage is the last figure on the line; look for the highest figure to see if your page file is large enough.

still boost performance by fixing the size and stopping Windows from wasting time by making the file larger and smaller as you open and close applications, which can fragment the page file and make it slower.

But before you change anything, you need to spend some time looking at how your memory is being used. How much memory do the applications you run actually need? Do you need more physical RAM or will making the page file larger be enough? Is Windows XP spending too much time swapping memory back and forth between RAM and the page file? That's called paging and it's a big drain on system performance.

Use the built-in tracking in Windows XP to see exactly how your system is running. Launch the programs you use the most. Open the Performance console from Administrative tools on the Performance and Maintenance Control Panel and pick the System Monitor from the tree on the left.

Click the Add button and choose Process as the Performance object and Working set as the counter, then pick each of the main programs you're running; this tells you how much memory each process is using.

Allocating memory

Even if you're not doing anything in an application, as long as it's open, that program is allocated a section of physical memory called the working set.

When you've got lots of free memory, Windows XP can allocate memory to new programs, but when you start to run out of memory it has to take memory from the working set of one program to give to another. Although the System Monitor graph makes it easy to compare figures, you'll get better results by setting up a log file to track the counters while you use your computer the way you usually do for a few hours.

Turn off disk space warnings if you use a whole partition for page file or you'll see this all the time

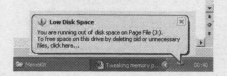

You can see the page file size in Explorer but you can't change it from here

In the left-hand pane of the Performance console under Performance Logs & Alerts, select Counter Logs then click in the right-hand pane and choose New log settings. Give the log file a name (include the date so you can compare different log files).

In the General tab select Add counters and add performance counters for the Paging File to see how Windows XP is using that; measure Percentage Usage and Percentage Usage Peak.

On the Log Files tab set the Log File Type to Text file (comma delimited). When you click OK, Windows XP starts logging the counters to the file; you'll see the log file go green in the list. Now use your PC as normal for a few hours, running different applications and opening files. Try running more demanding programs and take a note of what the time is, so you can see what shows up in the log file. But if you don't often use those programs, you're better off sticking to the programs you normally run, so you get a more accurate view.

When you're ready to look at the log, you'll find it in the C:\PerfLogs directory and you can open it in Notepad or Excel. The values at the end of each line are the percentages for how much of your page file is being used.

If these are more than 80 per cent each, you need to make the page file larger; if they're under 50 per cent you can reduce the initial size of the page file to the average size of the peak page file usage.

What's in the performance console

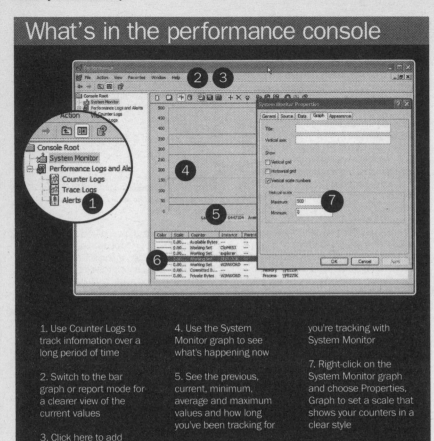

1. Use Counter Logs to track information over a long period of time

2. Switch to the bar graph or report mode for a clearer view of the current values

3. Click here to add more counters

4. Use the System Monitor graph to see what's happening now

5. See the previous, current, minimum, average and maximum values and how long you've been tracking for

6. The list of counters

you're tracking with System Monitor

7. Right-click on the System Monitor graph and choose Properties, Graph to set a scale that shows your counters in a clear style

Fast disk

Next, create another log file to measure the speed of the drive your page file is on. Add a counter for Memory, Pages/sec to show how many pages of memory have been swapped out to virtual memory or retrieved into real memory. A few disk hits per second is good but if it's over 20 you need to check whether it's the disk having problems or whether you just don't have enough RAM.

Add counters for Logical Disk, % Disk time and Physical Disk, Average Disk Queue Length; if they go up when the page speed goes down then it's your hard drive slowing

you down and you should move the page file to a faster disk.

If the page speed doesn't go down as the disk queue gets longer then Windows XP isn't waiting for virtual memory from disk – you just don't have enough RAM.

To see how much time paging is taking up, all you have to do is multiply the values from Memory, Pages/sec and Physical Disk, Average Disk sec/transfer. If the result is more than 0.1, this means that paging information between memory and disk accounts for 10 per cent of everything your hard drive is doing.

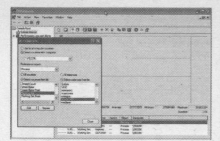

Use System Monitor to track how much memory particular applications use

All stop!

Before you start changing the page file settings, you need to change what Windows XP does if it crashes.

One of the ways Windows uses the page file is to store the contents of memory if your PC crashes and 'dump' that into a file so that you can look at the file to see what went wrong (or send it to Microsoft to look at). So the system failure settings affect how you can change the page file. What you choose also depends on whether you're putting your page file onto more than one hard drive.

Depending on the size of your hard drives and how many disk drives you have in your PC, you might want to use the whole of a drive for your Windows page file or split the page file between different disks.

By default, Windows XP puts the page file on the same drive as the rest of Windows, the one that your system boots from.

That means that Windows XP has to manage disk I/O for the Windows system directory and the page file from the same disk. Windows XP can handle multiple requests more efficiently if they're on different drives and if you split the page file itself between two drives, Windows XP can get information from both of them at once.

It also makes sense to put your page file on whichever disk is used least, as long as it's not a slower drive. Devoting a whole partition to the page file means the file won't get fragmented.

With other files on the disk, when the page file expands it can end up split into

Five top tools

■ PageDefrag
www.sysinternals.com
What it does Defragments the page file and other key system files to speed up your system.
What we think An excellent tool – it's tricky to do this by hand.

■ Cacheman
www.outertech.com
What it does Frees up memory at regular intervals and manages the disk cache (information Windows keeps in RAM for faster access, taking up memory you may want for applications).
What we think Handy tool to have.

■ RAM Idle
www.tweaknow.com/ramidl.html
What it does RAM Idle enables you to free up memory and manage the disk cache. You can also purge the clipboard and create shortcuts for applications that automatically free up memory when you start them.
What we think Another winner.

■ MemStat XP
www.memstat.prv.pl
What it does Frees up memory and shows you a graph of page file use; you can see figures or the chart as an icon in the System Tray.
What we think Again, you won't often need to recover memory with Windows XP but if you do, MemStat XP is easy to use and has lots of options.

■ MemoKit
www.memokit4all.com
What it does MemoKit monitors memory use and frees it up; you can get the same info in Windows XP but it's neatly presented with details of the memory and shared components.
What we think Free up memory or see what's going on – this is handy for both.

chunks which slows down transferring information back and forth. With only one drive you can get the same effect simply by fixing the size of the page file or defragmenting it regularly.

Don't confuse separate physical disks with multiple partitions on the same disk; putting the page file on a different partition on the same hard drive actually decreases performance because every time Windows XP writes to those files it has to swing the disk arm on the hard drive all the way over to that section and then back to where you're keeping your other files. It's more efficient for the disk arm to stay near the single page file.

You still need a small page file on the boot drive to capture important information if the system crashes, but Windows XP is smart enough to use the page file on the second hard drive because that isn't used as often as your main drive.

Right click on My Computer and select Properties, then the Advanced tab, followed by the Startup & Recovery Settings button. Under Write debugging information, pick how much information you want Windows XP to save in the memory dump file.

None means that Windows XP won't save any information at all, so it won't set any

minimum size for the page file, but you won't have important details if Windows crashes. Instead pick Small memory dump which saves only the minimum information and means you have to have a page file on your C: drive that's at least 2MB. Kernel memory dump needs 50MB and Complete memory dump needs a page file larger than your physical RAM so it can save everything in memory – you don't need these unless you're having problems with your PC. You'll need to restart your PC at this point.

Stop warnings

When you have the page file taking up a whole disk, you won't want to see the standard Windows warning that you're running out of disk space on that drive: normally you'd see that every five minutes when there's less than 50MB free so it would soon get irritating. You can turn off the warning completely in the Registry, but that would stop you getting a warning for the drive with your files on.

To do this, use Start, Run, REGEDIT to open the Registry editor, run System Restore and make a restore point in case you have problems. To turn off all disk space warnings go to HKEY_ CURRENT_USER\Software\ Microsoft\Windows\Current

STEP BY STEP

>> Changing the page file

1 RESIZE THE PAGE FILE
In System Properties choose Advanced, Performance, Settings, Advanced, Virtual Memory, Change. Put a small page file on your system drive if you want to track system crashes.

2 FIX THE PAGE FILE
Make the initial and maximum sizes the same and Windows XP won't spend time resizing the page file, which can fragment it. Pick Custom size and fill in the same figure for both sizes.

3 SPLIT THE PAGE FILE
Split your page file across more than one disk to speed it up; Windows can retrieve data from both. Pick the second and choose Custom size, then fill in the same page file sizes.

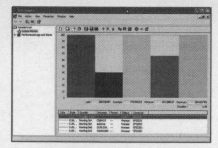

Change System Monitor to a bar graph, then right-click on the counters and choose Properties, Data, Colour to choose a colour for each counter

Version\Policies\Explorer\ and choose Edit, New, DWORD Value. Name the new value NoLowDiskSpaceChecks then double-click on it and set the Value data as 1.

More usefully, to turn off the warning for just the drive with your Page file on, go to HKEY_LOCAL_MACHINE\System\CurrentCon trolSet\Control\FileSystem\ and choose Edit, New, DWORD Value.

Name the value 'DisableLowDiskSpace Broadcast' and set the Value data to the number that matches your drive letter (A is 1, B is 2, C is 4, D is 8, etc).

Changing size

Now you can start changing your page file. Right-click on My Computer and select Properties; on the Advanced tab under Performance, click Settings and pick the Advanced tab again, then under Virtual Memory click Change. Your hard drives are listed at the top of the dialog, with the size of any page file.

Select the drive with the page file you want to change. Under 'Paging file size for selected drive', click 'Custom size and type' in the Initial size and then select Maximum size, in megabytes.

Fixing the size

It's a good idea to fix the size of the page file by making the initial and maximum sizes the same, otherwise Windows XP has to find more disk space as you need more virtual memory. If that space is in another part of the hard drive each time, the page file gets fragmented and is slower to access. Never

make the page file smaller than your RAM. If you've got less than 128MB of RAM, start with 1.75 times your real memory; if you've got more, start with 1.5 times your memory. You can make the page file bigger than that, depending on how much hard drive space you have available.

Click Set; if you're decreasing either size you'll need to restart your PC. To remove the page file on one drive, click 'No paging file'. To split the page file between disks, set the size on the first drive as half the total and the other half on the other drive.

In some circumstances you'll want to keep the initial and maximum sizes different. If you occasionally use a program that needs a lot of memory you want Windows XP to be able to increase the page file size to cope with it, but you won't need the page file to be that large all the time. That means the page file can get fragmented – speed it up again by defragmenting.

The simplest way to do this is with a utility called PageDefrag. This looks at the main system files and lets you defragment them the next time you restart your PC (or every time you restart your PC). It's worth running PageDefrag to check your system files once a month.

Alternatively, you can turn off the page file altogether by choosing 'No paging file' in the Virtual memory dialog and restarting your PC. Now defragment your hard drive (Accessories, System Tools, Disk Defragmenter) to make sure that there's plenty of continuous free space for Windows XP to put the page file in, so it's not fragmented from the start.

Windows XP can do a more thorough job of defragmenting your other files without the page file there as well. Now go back to the Virtual Memory dialog in System Properties and recreate the page file by choosing Custom size and setting the initial and maximum size.

Keep an eye on page file usage as you use software; right-click on your counter log in the Performance console and choose Properties, Schedule and set it to run again in three months' time so you can make sure that your page file is still the right size for the way you work.

Microsoft Management Console

Inside the Microsoft Management Console

The MMC is a console you can use to build a kind of Windows XP toolkit. Add or remove various resources at your leisure for an individualised set of system tools.

While Windows XP does the hard work of keeping your PC running smoothly, there are a lot of tools that let you see what programs are running and how well they're performing – and enable you to make changes.

That's what the Microsoft Management Console (MMC) is for: it isn't an administration tool itself, it's an interface for organising other tools. Some of the tools are ones you can get at in other ways, like Device Manager. Others you can only view in a management console – either one of the default consoles supplied with Windows XP or a custom console you put together. Let's take a look at what it's all about.

If you right-click on My Computer and choose Manage, you'll get a console with sets of tools already added in: you'll find other consoles on the Administrative Tools menu (right-click on the taskbar and choose Properties, Start Menu, Customize, Advanced and scroll down to the System Administrative Tools section if you don't see them on the Start menu).

These consoles are locked so you can't add or remove any of the tools, but you can create your own. This is useful because it means you can create selections of tools and utilities you can access from one easy to locate place.

Just choose Start, Run and type in MMC to get a blank console. Then choose File, Add/Remove Snap-in to add the tools you want. (The tools you can use inside the MMC are called snap-ins, because when you add them they 'snap' into place.)

Some of the snap-ins come with Windows XP, others come as parts of programs that need a lot of administration. You can also add in links to useful Web pages. And you can add in any program that runs as an ActiveX control, for example the System Monitor or NetMeeting. As you add more snap-ins to your console, the Help files for those snap-ins are linked to the Help file for your console, so you don't have to hunt around for the information.

Extensions

Some snap-ins have extensions – extra options that you can choose to load or turn off. If you're including the Computer Management snap-in, this includes other snap-ins as extensions so if you already have tools like the Device Manager elsewhere in the tree, you can turn them off inside Computer Management. You'll find the options for any snap-in that has extensions on the Extensions tab of the Add/Remove Snap-in dialog.

Use File, Save to save your console and it automatically shows up on the Administrative Tools menu. The file type is .MSC, which stands for Management Saved Console and to help your console stand out, you can use File, Options, Change Icon to pick the icon that will appear in the menu, in the corner of the console and when you Alt-Tab between applications. You can name your console here too, to distinguish it from the built-in tools. And once you've got the tools you want, you might want to change the Console mode from the same dialog.

Setting up the tools you want in MMC

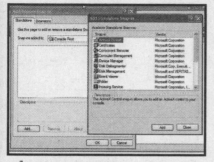

1 ADD IN YOUR CHOICES
Go through the list and add in the tools you want to work with: you can always remove them later if you don't use them

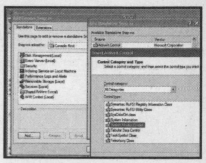

2 ADDING ACTIVEX
You can add ActiveX controls to the console, so you can link to any tool that works as a control even if it's not on the list

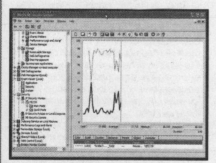

3 SYSTEM MONITOR
We've added the System Monitor Control as a quick way to see specific performance measurements

4 ADDING WEB PAGES
Add handy Web pages – like the Microsoft Security update page at www.microsoft.com /security/ – so you can jump to them quickly

MORE MMC HELP
Go to the Help and Support Centre within Windows XP

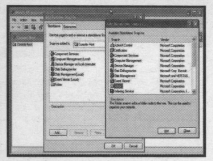

5 GETTING ORGANISED
If you want to organise the tools, add Folders from here, then right-click in the console tree to name the folders what you want

6 PICKING YOUR TARGET
Now go back to the Add/remove Snap-in dialog, pick the new folder as target and add the tools you want – you can't drag and drop them

The right mode

When you create a console, you're working in Author mode, which enables you to add and remove snap-ins, make new windows and build taskpads. However, if you share your computer with other people, you might want to let them check on performance or defragment the disk but not change drive letters or stop and start services. The solution is User mode which prevents the addition of snap-ins that you've not already included. And you can't accidentally remove any of the tools either, so it's a safer mode to work in even if you don't share your PC.

Give your console a name and pick an icon for it: you can save it as an .msc file

User mode, full access lets you see all the snap-ins and create new windows. If you've arranged everything neatly, you can lock the arrangement by switching to User mode, limited access. This multiple window lets you see only the parts of the console tree that were expanded when you saved it, which enables you to lock out some of the low-level options on tools without removing the whole tool.

You can also use the View, Customize command to remove menus, the console tree, the toolbars, the status bar or the description at the top, giving you a very simple interface for particular tools. Beware of removing the Standard menus (Action and View) option though: once you've done that it's not easy to get back to the Customize View dialog to add them again.

You can create one console with all the tools you want to use, organised into folders, or different consoles for different tasks.

You can also change the view, from a single window to tiled windows for several tools at once. From the Windows menu: right-click on any of the tools in the console tree and choose New Windows from Here to get multiple windows to tile.

Extra commands

You can add extra commands to a tool by making a taskpad.

Right-click on the snap-in you want to create a taskpad for and choose New Taskpad View. This runs the New Taskpad View wizard and lets you choose whether you want a vertical or horizontal list – you can change just the tool you're working with or all the tools that have the same layout. You can see reminders and handy information as text at the side of the list or as Info Tips when you hover the mouse over them.

You can change the name of the taskpad if you find the name of the tool isn't always clear, or if you want to make several different taskpads for the same tool, with different extras and layouts: it's also worth typing in a description.

Once you've finished the New Taskpad View wizard, you'll see the New Tasks wizard, which lets you add the commands. If there's a command on the right-click menu of a tool you use a lot, pick the menu command option to make it a link in the detail pane so it's easier to use. You can link to other tools by picking links you've saved as favourites. And you can link to other programs like System Information or Scheduled Tasks by adding a Shell command.

Shell commands are very versatile: you can include anything that you can type into the Run box on the Start menu so you can use them to link to Web pages or to run scripts using the Windows Scripting Host.

Making utilities

Adding commands to a snap-in makes useful utilities; use File, Save As to save a copy of the console and delete the rest of the snap-ins then close the console tree. Choose View, Filter if you want to focus in on the crucial information: for example, in the System section of the Event Log you'll want to see Errors and Warnings but you can skip the Information events unless you want to look at a specific service in action.

To save information from a tool, choose Save as Text File from the Action menu in the console window. You won't see this option for all tools, if there isn't any information you can usefully save, but it's ideal for saving a list of IRQ settings for reference or printing out startup errors so you can refer to them while you're rebooting.

If you're tracking a lot of performance indicators and the built-in graphs don't give you enough flexibility, choose Export List from the Action menu to save the information as a tab- or comma-delimited file that you can load into Microsoft Excel.

You can sort the details into any order you like, lay it out in a pivot table, or create sophisticated graphs to analyse trends.

>> Creating a taskpad

1 GETTING STARTED
Choose how you want to see the list of information by right-clicking on the snap-on, selecting New Taskpad view

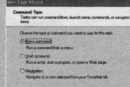

2 ADDING COMMAND
Add extra commands to the taskpad: you can run programs, link to Web pages or jump to other snap-ins

3 PICKING AN ICON
Pick an icon for the command you're adding: you can choose an icon with the right meaning or one you think matches best

Creating consoles

Customise the management tools to get exactly the information you need about your system

Windows XP is rather like a swan; it looks serene and graceful on the surface but underneath, services, processes, drivers and programs are all running like mad to get you where you want to go. Unless something actually goes wrong, you'll never see any of this – unless you look.

With the tools in the Microsoft Management Console (MMC) you can tune up the performance of your system, check that everything is running smoothly or just learn more about how it works.

The MMC is an interface that lets you combine exactly the tools you need in one convenient place (called a console).

There are some handy consoles that come with Windows XP but you can put together your own selection, including handy web pages and ActiveX controls as well as the standard 'snap-in' tools (so called because they 'snap' into place in the console interface).

Build your own console

Open an empty console by choosing Start, Run, MMC and use File, Add/Remove Snap-ins to pick the tools to include.

The snap-ins on your list will vary depending on the software you've installed; some applications include snap-ins that let you control options and you'll find ActiveX controls you've downloaded with web pages

here as well.

Other snap-ins let you control and monitor Windows XP itself. You can find many of them on the standard Windows consoles (Administrative Tools in the Performance and Maintenance control panel) and it's worth loading up Computer Management which has many of the tools in, so you can see how they work.

Now start building your own. For monitoring your storage, start with the obvious tools like Disk Defragmenter and Disk Management, which lets you format drives, change drive letters and see how much disk space you've got left. It would be handy to add Disk Cleanup as well, so you can delete unnecessary temporary files to regain disk space.

It's not listed as a snap-in, so we'll make a taskpad that includes the command.

Making a taskpad

Choose Action, New Taskpad view and follow the steps in the wizard. Fortunately, you can stick with the defaults for most settings. You can choose to use the taskpad just for the top level of your console or for every level that accepts it.

Once you've created the taskpad the New Task wizard pops up. Pick Shell command to run a program like Disk Cleanup. If you don't know where the actual program is or what it's called, open the Start

Building a Security & Updates Console

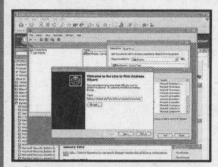

1 LINK TO SECURITY SITES
Choose File, Add/Remove Snap-in, Link to web page, and fill in the URL; give the web page a name. We're including Microsoft security bulletins, CERT advisories and other online info, as well as the Certificates snap-in.

2 ORGANISE YOUR CONSOLE
Let's divide our links into two folders; choose File, Add/ Remove Snap-in, Folder, then close the boxes, right-click on the folder in the console tree and pick Rename. Now go to File, Add/ Remove Snap-in and select a folder.

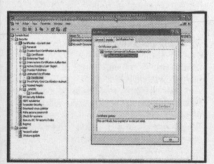

3 IDENTIFY CERTIFICATES
Digital certificates tell you who the bearer is and who identifies them. You'll mostly come across them as you download controls from the web. The Certificates snap-in lets you look back at the certificates you've accepted and whether they're valid.

4 ORGANISE CERTIFICATES
As you add snap-ins to the console you get extra commands on the menus. View, Options lets you switch the certificates snap-in from showing a list organised by who authorises certificates to a list of what the certificates are for, like signing email.

MORE ABOUT THE MMC

http://www.microsoft.com/technet/treeview/default.asp?url=/technet/
prodtechnol/windows2000serv/howto/mmcsteps.asp

5 **SAVE YOUR CONSOLE**
Choose File, Save. Windows XP saves your new console in the Administrative tools menu but you can move it if you prefer. Right-click and Rename to change the first branch of the console tree from console root.

6 **MAKE A TASKPAD**
Select console root and choose Action, New Taskpad View; choose a vertical list and pick the defaults. Use the Task Wizard to add tasks like running your anti-virus software then use View, Customise to get rid of parts you don't need.

menu, find the shortcut and right-click on it to choose Properties and find the file name. Disk Cleanup is actually C:\WINDOWS\System32\cleanmgr.exe; most of the accessories are in the System32 directory.

Add more tasks by choosing Action, Edit Taskpad View, Tasks, New. You can include third-party programs and utilities here.

Information in the Event Viewer will often be surprising because Windows XP doesn't show you error messages for issues that happen during startup or shutdown

Taskpads are a handy way of bringing everything together; it's easy to forget which utilities you've got with a big package like Norton SystemWorks.

Other useful storage snap-ins include the Indexing service which lets you search for files. It's more detailed than the standard Search Assistant and you can change which directories it covers from here.

Making backups

Taking backups on a CD burner lets you store a lot of data quickly and cheaply; 650MB for less than 50p will store a lot of documents.

But when you've got a lot of discs it's hard to keep track, especially if you don't write more than the date on them. The Removable Storage snap-in keeps a list of CDs or tapes that you've used.

Got a network at home? Add in the Shared Folders tool to keep track of which folders you've shared out, who's connecting to them and what files they've got open.

Once you've added the snap-ins and

commands you want, use File, Save; by default Windows XP adds your console to the Administrative Tools menu in the All programs menu, but you can put the file anywhere you want. Use File, Options, 'Console user mode' to lock the console so you don't accidentally delete any of the snap-ins while you're using it.

Safe and secure

There are some excellent security resources on the web. On Microsoft's site you can read the latest security bulletins and check your PC with the Personal Security Advisor. Other sites will check whether you're exposed to hackers. Add in your anti-virus software and you can be pretty well protected.

Put them all in a console together and you'll find it easier to check your system regularly. For a full guide on how to do this just turn back to page 27.

Tip-top condition

Windows XP enables you to track every detail of system performance. You can do it in real time with the System Monitor,

zooming in on details about memory, disk, processor, network, and other activity and adding counters for everything from how well the file system cache is working to how many interrupts the processor deals with and how much processor time and memory individual applications take up. It shows you much more detail than the Task Manager.

Use Performance Logs to track the information over a longer time and save it to a file or to set alerts to see a notification if a specific performance statistic shows up at any time.

The System Monitor and Performance Logs are both in the standard Performance console, but if you choose to make your own you can add a handy spreadsheet control so you can analyse the figures quickly. You can also add in the Disk Defragmenter, then if your results show your PC is slow, defragmenting is the first thing to try to speed it up.

To compare your PC speed to other machines, you need benchmarking software. There's an excellent list at the website Benchmark HQ (www.benchmarkhq.ru/

STEP BY STEP

>> What to put in your own Performance console

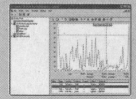

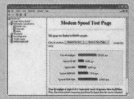

1 **MONITOR YOUR SYSTEM** Add the same tools as the standard Windows XP Performance console: System Monitor ActiveX and Performance Logs snap-in. Disk Defragmenter is useful to have. If you have Excel, add in the Spreadsheet ActiveX. We've set up some counters in System Performance; let them run then choose Copy Properties.

2 **ANALYSE THE FIGURES** You don't always want to go to the bother of setting up a log to compare counters but you want to check the figures closely. Paste them in the Spreadsheet control: you'll find it's much quicker than launching Excel. You get a lot of information about each counter, including the minimum, maximum and

3 **USE OTHER TOOLS** We've added in some web performance tests for checking how fast your modem is; there are plenty of websites that give you figures like this (try http://hom epage.ntlworld.com/dgilbert/ testpage.htm or http://bandwi dthplace .com/speedtest/) that you copy into the spreadsheet and export to Excel to check your ISP isn't slowing down.

english.html): you should also check out PassMark performance test (www.passmark.com) and SiSoftware Sandra (www.sisoftware.demon.co.uk/sandra/).

Adding them

Make a taskpad view and add these to your Performance console and you'll have something to compare your results to, letting

you judge your PC's performance.

Consoles also enable you to track the services that Windows runs in the background; use the Services snap-in to see what's going on. These are dozens of low-level processes that start automatically when you turn on your PC.

Windows XP runs a standard set of services to let you do things like print, play

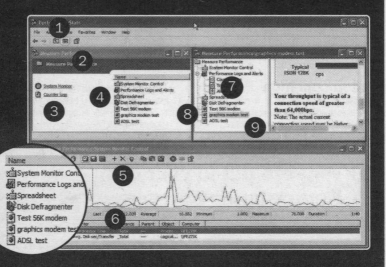

Organising Your Console

Use multiple windows and taskpads to get all the commands you need in your console and see them at the same time

1. Add snap-ins and run snap-in commands from the menu.

2. Create a taskpad to add programs and navigation buttons to your console.

3. Navigate to other sections of the console.

4. You can tell from the icon that System Monitor

Control and Spreadsheet are ActiveX controls.

5. Add counters to track specific aspects of performance in the System Monitor Control.

6. Add counters to track specific aspects of performance in the System Monitor Control.

7. Use Performance Logs and Alerts to track counters over a longer time and save the results in a file.

8. Link to web pages and see them inside the console.

9. Navigate from the console tree or turn it off to see a tool better.

Event viewer alerts and performance log files all have dates on, but if you need to jog your memory on which day a file refers to, use File, Add/Remove Snap-in, ActiveX and add in the Calendar Control

Use View, Filter to screen out information and Success and Failure audits (you don't see them in Windows XP Home Edition anyway) and the errors and warnings are easier to work with

music, burn CDs and connect to a network if you want.

Turn off the services you don't need

Not everyone will need all of those services; if you don't have a printer or a CD burner, or you're not connected to a network, you can turn those services off until you do need them, which may improve performance.

Of course you shouldn't disable key processes of the operating system: you definitely need the services that manage process scheduling, interrupt handling, file management, virtual memory management and tuning the system automatically. But there are plenty of other, less critical services that are started by default that may not need to be running, depending on how you use your computer.

First, use System Restore to set a restore point before you change anything, in case you have problems later. Now look in the Service snap-in and sort the list by Startup Type; ignore any services that are started manually.

Look at our list of services you may not need in the Expert Tip box below; before you make any changes, right-click on the service and choose Properties, Dependencies to see if other services use this service.

You might not think you need Terminal Services unless you're connecting to

other machines over a network, but actually you need it for making use of Fast User Switching on your PC.

Experiment with changing the Startup type to manual on Properties, General.

Never disable a service; if another process needs the service, it can start it up. Juts go back to your Performance console to check the difference disabling the services makes.

Quick access

The programs you use every day, like email and your web browser, are on the Start menu, but you can put your console there too. Even though you can search through the Help and Support Centre for the utilities you don't need as often, building your own console with exactly the right selection of tools makes it easier to maintain your system – and the information you glean from the snap-ins will help you work out what you need to do.

Jargon explained

■ Console
The Microsoft Management Console is the tool you use for building collections of tasks and tools. The console is the interface that you collect your tasks in.

System Properties

38 System Properties and the Device Manager

How to easily configure, adjust and enhance hardware performance, and check that it's working!

39 A quick guide to System Properties

A simple look at the many useful options you can take advantage of.

41 Creating new hardware profiles

A step by step guide to copying, selecting and editing your PC's hardware profiles.

System addict!

No longer just about the Device Manager, the System Properties Control Panel has a whole host of extra, essential features in it...

J ust as some people would never dream of tinkering under the bonnet of their car, the same is true of System Properties in Windows found in the Control Panel. Because it lies at the very heart of the operating system, controlling a number of vital elements, you would only be entering its realms if you were trying to fix a particular problem or if you were an enthusiast looking to tweak a setting or two.

Those of you who have upgraded to Windows XP from a previous incarnation of Windows will notice that there are a few extra tabs present. In the past the focus of System Properties was really the Device Manager, but now there's a lot more to it.

As well as configuring hardware and making sure that it's working correctly there are new settings that can be adjusted to enhance performance. System Restore and Remote Assistance features have been added as well.

This in-depth guide aims to demystify this area of Windows XP and explain its function in more detail.

Hardware

System Properties' only real concern is hardware. Other aspects such as Users and Software are handled elsewhere in Control Panel by User Accounts and Add or Remove Programs respectively. When you add a new piece of hardware to your PC in the majority of cases plug and play will kick in and the item should be recognised as soon as the item is plugged in or when your PC is rebooted. Alternatively, use the manufacturer's installation CD that came with the device and insert that in your drive.

If your new hardware isn't automatically recognised or you don't have a CD then you can add the item manually yourself. From the Hardware tab click on Add Hardware Wizard and follow the step by step guide. Windows XP will search your PC for new items of hardware or you can manually select the type of hardware device you want to add. As well as the common items such as Printers, Network Cards or Tape Drives you can also add COM Ports or Printer Ports. This can come in handy should you have a piece of hardware such as an internal modem that you are having problems installing.

To be able to install the drivers for a new piece of hardware you need to be logged into

System Properties quick guide

You can use System Properties to manage basic settings, for example, the name of your computer on a network right up to more advanced options such as applying limits for the paging file. Alternatively, select the Advanced tab and click on Performance and you'll be able to apportion processor and memory usage to different

areas of Windows XP. Some of the old features have become more accessible and there are some new features too, such as Remote Access. Here's our quick guide to what else you can find under System Properties.

■ Make sure your PC stays in tip top condition by receiving regular notification of any updates available.

■ One of the many new innovative features included within Windows XP is Remote Assistance.

■ This will give you a quick rundown on the specs of your PC and the type of operating system.

■ You only need to give your PC a name if it's part of a network, so unless you're linked up, leave it blank.

■ Manage your hardware. From here you can add new items of hardware and update device drivers.

■ Use this tab to adjust settings that will affect the performance and appearance of Windows XP.

■ When you run into problems, System Restore lets you backtrack to a trouble-free point in time.

≫ Hardware installation tips

There may not always be a Windows XP driver available for your hardware device. Before giving up though, make sure that you've searched the manufacturer's website thoroughly and tried the likes of www.driverguide.com. Don't despair though if you can't find anything because in most cases the Windows 2000 drivers for that device should work OK.

When installing hardware devices

such as additional hard disks or CD ROM drives, one of the most common causes of them not working is a result of incorrect jumper settings.

For example, if you're installing a CD Writer to work alongside your DVD drive, one of them will need to be set to Master and the other to Slave. As long as you set the jumper to Master on one of the drives there's no need to set a jumper on the other drive.

an user account with administrator-level access. If you're using an account that doesn't have these and you try to install drivers you'll be asked for an administrator's password during setup.

Hardware Profiles

Every time your computer starts up, it loads a Hardware Profile which contains details of the hardware configuration and device drivers that Windows XP will be using. You can create different Hardware Profiles which enable you to run different hardware configurations on the same machine. You can choose which profile to use at startup.

There are a number of occasions when this type of capability comes in useful. For example, if you don't use a particular piece of hardware too often then you can configure a profile and have that device enabled or disabled to suit you. This way you can save on system resources when you don't need to use it. Another instance would be if you use a laptop and a docking station.

The indication here shows that there are no drivers installed for both devices

Depending on whether it's attached means you'll be using different pieces of hardware. You may only be able to use an item such as a tape drive or printer when the docking station is attached. Hardware Profiles would come in especially useful here enabling you to select the configuration you require, avoiding the need to configure the devices and drivers every time.

Device Manager

For information about all the individual items of hardware that are installed on your PC you can use Device Manager. As well as conveniently listing hardware by device type it can also reveal if a particular item is working correctly or not. If a symbol such as a question mark or exclamation mark is displayed next to a device it can indicate that it's not working correctly.

To see exactly what the problem is, just click on the + sign next to the category and then double click on the item. Under Device Status there should be a brief description of what is causing the trouble and how it can be rectified. If it's a driver problem, select the Driver tab to either update the driver with a new version or roll back the driver to the working version that was installed previously.

Changing views

As well as viewing which items of hardware are installed by 'type' they can also be listed by which connection they are using. If you need to know how your machine is configured this can save you the trouble of opening up this your PC. For example, you'll be able to view the IDE channels and see which drives are connected to which channel.

You'll also be able to check how many PCI devices are installed and if you have any free slots available for extra ones.

When you view the properties of some devices you will see that they have an Advanced tab as well. For example, with a modem the Advanced option enables you to improve performance by altering port settings and adding additional initialisation strings to it.

Driver Signing

In previous versions of Windows it was possible to install any old driver. The operating system would allow you to do this, even though it may not have been the correct file and the device may not have functioned properly as a result. With Windows XP the installation of drivers is a much more controlled affair.

The introduction of signed drivers means that if you see a driver carrying that logo it means that it's been thoroughly tested by Microsoft. It will be free from viruses and is extremely unlikely to make your system lock up or crash.

Due to the risks associated with installing an unsigned driver a warning will appear on screen when you attempt this.

Take a chance

You may need to get a piece of hardware working at all costs and the only driver you have is an unsigned one. Windows XP will automatically set a system restore point whenever you install an unsigned driver so if your PC does get a little temperamental afterwards, you can still revert to a working system. You should back up all your important files beforehand, just in case.

For those of you confident in your ability to install hardware and deal with drivers, you can change the way in which warnings appear. With the Hardware tab selected, click on Driver Signing under Device Manager and set your preference. You can choose to have Windows XP ignore the fact that a driver is unsigned. Alternatively, by selecting Warn you will receive an alert but you will be able to override the warning if you want to. Block means that only signed drivers can be installed on your PC.

>> Creating a new Hardware Profile

1 CREATE A NEW PROFILE The easiest way to create a new Hardware Profile is to copy an existing one. To do this click on Copy and a duplicate will be made. Then highlight each of the Profiles and click on Properties. Go down to Hardware profiles selection, check the box 'Always include this profile as an option when Windows starts' and click OK.

2 SELECTING YOUR PROFILE You can set a default profile to load each time Windows starts or you can select from a menu. To set a default, use the arrow buttons to make sure your preferred option is the one that's at the top of the list. If you want a choice, under Hardware profiles selection check 'Wait until I select a hardware profile'.

3 EDIT A PROFILE Next, restart your PC and select the profile that you want to change. Go into Device Manager and locate an item of hardware. Right click on it. You should now choose Disable or Enable in order to make it inactive or active within your current profile. When you're finished, simply close the Device Manager.

Understanding Virtual Memory

In this chapter we explore the features of the Advanced tab and look at how you manage profiles, improve performance and enhance the Windows XP interface

We've looked at the Hardware section of System Properties and the ways in which you can use it to deal with your installed hardware more effectively. Now we continue our in-depth examination of System Properties by taking a look at the features contained under the Advanced tab.

Although the tab is labelled 'Advanced', don't let this put you off from taking a look and adjusting any settings. Here you'll find tools that let you manage performance, adjust profile settings and deal with startup problems and system information.

Never before has an operating system given a user such control over all areas of their computer. As well as working in conjunction with your software applications you can actually apply settings that allocate a percentage of processor usage to a particular program or task. You can also optimise the Windows XP interface for appearance and performance.

Performance vs looks

The features under the Advanced tab give you control over three key areas of your operating system: Performance, User Profiles and Startup and Recovery. The Performance section is split into two areas, Visual Effects and Advanced. The first of these deals mainly with the Windows XP interface and gives you numerous options on how you can make it appear.

Check a few boxes and add some great new effects to your interface

If your PC only just meets or isn't far above the minimum system requirements for Windows XP then you'll find this part of the operating system particularly useful. You'd be surprised how much of your PC's resources are taken up by the graphically intensive effects you see on the interface, for example, shadows on text and animations when performing tasks such as copying files and folders.

Depending on the specification of your PC you can either use the Visual Effects tab to optimise your interface for appearance and aesthetic appeal or you can select the options that will ensure you get the best performance from your PC. The default setting is 'Let Windows choose what's best for my computer' along with three other options. The first two are pretty self explanatory, and selecting either check box will enable you to adjust for best performance or appearance.

The third option is Custom which gives you the opportunity to choose the individual appearance settings that you would like to use. In the past you've probably been blissfully unaware of how your computer's menus and buttons appear and perform. However, scroll down the list of check boxes and you'll see the kind of effects you've been using up until now, along with some of those you haven't.

There are some interesting options here that will bring cool effects to the Windows XP interface. The trade-off is extra use of your system's resources.

Those who have recently purchased a new PC should have nothing to worry about in this area, but those with a system of around two years' or so old whose specification isn't as high would probably be better off adjusting their Performance

Options to enhance the running of their system, rather than its appearance.

Processor power

Now you've optimised the way Windows XP looks, it's time to move on to the way in which it deals with your installed software. Click on the Advanced tab under Performance Options and the first setting you'll see is Processor scheduling. By default, Windows XP allocates the majority of its processor time to programs rather than background tasks. You can speed up other tasks you may be carrying out by checking the Background services option.

There's no harm experimenting with the option to find out which one works best for you. The Memory usage option enables you to choose between Programs or your System cache for the lion's share of its resource. It's set to Programs but anyone who uses cache hungry editing software for graphics, audio or video should select 'System cache'.

Understanding Virtual Memory

The final option under the Performance Options Advanced tab is Virtual Memory. When your system is performing its tasks and is running low on memory it turns to your hard drive for help. A proportion of your hard drive is then used to simulate normal system RAM, hence the name Virtual Memory. Just to confuse you, it's also known as the swap file or paging file. The amount of space it uses is usually around 1.5 times the amount of RAM

you have in your PC. Its filename is pagefile.sys and it's stored in the same folder as your system files, usually the root of your main drive. You can change the size of your paging file along with its location.

Does size matter?

Windows sets the size of the paging file automatically. However, if you have a large amount of RAM installed on your PC, say more than 256MB, but don't really use it,

Top Tip

■ Just because you have plenty of RAM installed on your PC don't think that you can do away with your pagefile.sys completely. Windows XP, along with other applications, requires it to be present on your system otherwise you could find yourself getting rather a lot of 'out of memory' error messages.

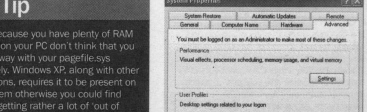

Select the Advanced tab to manage Performance, User Profiles and Startup and Recovery Options

STEP BY STEP

>> Changing the location of the paging file

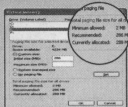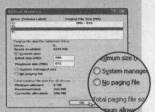

1 **GO TO VIRTUAL MEMORY**
Log in as Administrator then go into System Properties, select the Advanced tab and click on Settings. Click on the Advanced tab under Performance Options, go to Virtual Memory and click Change. Your C: drive should be highlighted showing an amount for the Paging File.

2 **CHOOSE A NEW DRIVE**
Select the new location of the paging file. Go down to 'Total paging file size for all drives' and there will be a 'Recommended' figure. Check Custom size and then enter this figure next to Initial size. Enter a limit next to Maximum size as well, usually double the Initial size amount.

3 **MAKE THE CHANGE**
Under Drive, click on C: again and check the box 'No paging file'. A warning message will appear about debugging information. Click on Yes to continue, keep clicking OK and you'll be asked to restart your computer. Your paging file will be moved when your PC boots up.

then it's worth reducing the size of your paging file and reclaiming some hard drive space. If you do make a change and memory error messages appear, you'll know you've set a size that's too low.

Someone who has a small amount of RAM may wish to consider increasing the size of their paging file. The default setting is 1.5 times the amount of installed RAM, up to a maximum of three times. There's no hard and fast rule as to how big you should set the paging file. Try several settings above the default and monitor performance.

To change the size of your paging file, click in the Initial size (MB): box and enter a new figure. Try two times your RAM and then double this figure for the Maximum size (MB): box. You then need to restart your PC. Alternatively, Windows XP can alter the size of the paging file for you 'on the fly'. Check the 'System managed size' option to do this but check how much hard drive is in use.

Another way to improve performance is to free up system resources and move your paging file to another drive. This must be a separate drive, not just a different partition.

Managing User Profiles

Any amendments you need to make to individual logins will be carried out through the User Accounts option under Control Panel. The User Profiles section under the Advanced tab in System Properties gives details of all the user accounts that have been created, along with how much hard drive space they use.

You should always use this to manage your users rather than going directly to any folders in My Computer and amending folders there.

From User Profiles you will be able to manage your profiles correctly by deleting or copying them accordingly. If a profile isn't being used any more you can just highlight it and click on Delete to remove it from Windows XP. Using this method ensures that any associated files and registry settings are removed as well.

Here's one we made earlier

The 'Copy To' option makes it easy to create another login that has the same permissions as an existing user. If you have set up a complicated set of access rights, rather than set this up all over again, you can just duplicate one you made earlier and then rename it.

Startup and recovery

This area of Windows XP enables you to manage how your PC starts, whether it's by selecting one of a number of operating systems or a recovery option. When you boot your PC you're given the option to choose which operating system you would like to use. The time limit for making your choice is set to 30 seconds but you can change this figure if you need to. If you would like the default operating system to start each time then just clear the first check box. You can also select a time limit for selecting from the recovery options list.

When a problem occurs with a piece of hardware or a software application, Windows XP displays a Stop Error on screen. In some cases, after the error has been displayed, the system will restart automatically. To stop this from happening you should go down to System failure and uncheck Automatically restart. You'll then be able to make any necessary changes to Windows XP and restart the PC yourself.

The 'Write debugging information' section contains settings for how error details are stored on your computer. If a technician is trying to resolve an error on your machine, he may ask you to switch between memory dump options as the various options store different information.

Environment variables

Environment variables contain the information that a task requires in order to perform a certain behaviour. For example, should any applications wish to use the temp file, the variable defines its actual location, usually, c:\windows\temp.

Environment variables differ between computers, but along with the location of the temp file you should be able to edit paths to

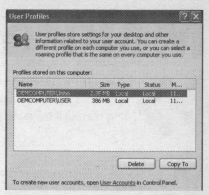

The easiest way to create a profile is to copy an existing one

system files along with IRQs for items of hardware (the IRQ, or interrupt request line, is the line over which devices can send interrupt signals to your PC).

Error reporting

When Windows XP encounters a problem or if an application terminates prematurely you will have noticed a small window pop up informing you that a log of the error has been created. Click on Error Reporting and you'll be able to choose whether or not to use this feature and if so to restrict it to the operating system and/or programs.

Assuming that you do receive an error and you click on Send Error Report, where do you think the report goes to? The cynics would say a black hole and that nobody actually deals with it. However, they would be wrong. All such error reports are sent straight off to oca.microsoft.com and then analysed by Microsoft.

Alternatively, you can send reports manually by going to the oca.microsoft.com site and clicking on Submit. The site then performs a quick search of your system and any error reports that have been created recently are displayed on screen. You can then select which of the error reports you would like to send and press 'Send'.

That's not the end of the story either. Click on Status and you'll be able to check what's happening with any of your submissions and view any comments that have been made.

Maintenance

The System Control panel makes it a cinch to keep your computer bang up to date – or restore it to normal if things should go horribly wrong

Windows XP is your flexible friend: it provides all sorts of tools for adjusting its settings, such as System Properties, which we've been exploring here. In the last part, we'll focus on updating your software to prevent crashes and restoring your system if the worst does happen. First, though, we've time for a quick tour of System Properties' nooks and crannies.

The first tab you see when opening the System Properties window is General. Although taken for granted by many, it displays details of your setup. You know you're running Windows XP, but General lists the version number – helpful for diagnosing

system faults. Your processor and available memory are also shown here.

There's also a note of who this copy of Windows XP is registered to, a piece of information you can change by editing the Registry. This isn't normally necessary, but if a PC changes hands then the name of the registered owner will have to be altered. A company may wish to add a logo or contact details for support purposes – again, it's possible to edit this in the Registry. Go to HKEY_LOCAL_MACHINE\SOFTWARE\Micros oft\Windows NT\CurrentVersion and change the name under RegisteredOwner.

If altering Strings and DWORD values isn't your cup of tea, try Customizer XP: it

STEP BY STEP

>> Using Customizer XP

1 CHANGE WINDOWS LOGO
Right click on My Computer and choose Properties. Under the General tab you'll see a Windows logo next to your system information. To change this logo in Customizer XP, by click on OEM Info under System Tools and select your own image.

2 CHANGE OWNER INFO
Under Registry Tweak, click on System. Check the box next to Change Windows Owner Information, and you'll be able to change details of the Registered Owner and Registered Organization without having to delve into the Registry yourself.

3 TWEAK EVERYTHING!
As well as Registry adjustments, Customizer XP enables you to alter other areas of your system. For example, you can adjust your RAM settings, remove Control Panel icons you don't use and allocate application priority for processor usage.

takes the worry out of making changes to your system. The program contains over 80 tweaks, and the interface makes light work of advanced system adjustments.

Computer Name

When Windows XP is first installed, you are asked to enter a name and description for your PC. Leaving the name section blank will result in a default name being inserted. You don't need to worry about either area unless you connect your PC to a network, at which time you'll have to give it a name so it can be identified by other PCs on the network.

If you have two PCs on your network, call one 'Dad's PC' and the other 'Family PC'. The description isn't vital for network operation, although you can use it to state the specification or location of a particular machine: for example, STUDY PC PIII 750. You can rename your PC at any time by clicking on Change under the General tab.

Using System Restore

W hen all else fails the System Restore utility is a godsend. In the past the only tool that Windows users could rely on was Scanreg. This would enable you to revert back to a previously working copy of the Registry. However, for other data it would be a case of relying on backups that had been made and recovering other files from there.

Going Back

With System Restore it's possible to go back to a given point in time when everything worked, and restore all your files. Don't think you'll never have to back up again, though. Backups are the only way to compensate you against the likes of a complete hardware failure or the loss of your machine through theft.

System Restore should be used when you've made a mistake configuring Windows XP and you're unable to undo the changes. Alternatively, you may find your PC isn't quite working as it should

---

STEP BY STEP

≫ Exclude a folder from the Restore process

1 EDIT THE REGISTRY
The Registry already contains details of certain files and folders that are excluded from the process. Open the Registry Editor and locate the Key HKEY_LOCAL_MACHINE\ SYSTEM\CurrentControlSet\ Control\BackupRestore\ FilesNotToBackup.

2 CREATE A NEW KEY
Once you have located this, right click on it and choose Edit, New, Multi-String Value. You'll now need to create a new Key for your folder. For reference purposes, give it a name you will recognise and remember, for example the folder name itself.

3 EDIT THE VALUE
Next, right click on your new Key and choose Modify. Then under Value data, enter the full path to your particular folder. When you're done, click on OK. This won't actually come into effect until you create the next Restore Point.

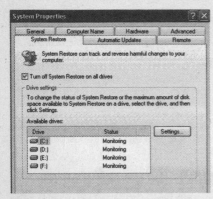

Turning off System Restore will delete any existing restore points on that particular drive

Customizer XP

■ Download Customizer XP from www.tweaknow.com/netopt.html. Once installed, you'll see a number in your system tray. This is the amount of free RAM available. Watch this figure to see when your system resources are getting low.

following the installation of a particular software application.

Configuration
Select the System Restore tab to begin configuring its options. Using System Restore has a price – hard drive space.

By default it will have earmarked some of the space on every partition you have set up on your PC, around 10% of free space. You can see how much drive space has been swallowed up by clicking on the Settings button.

Fortunately, you can choose which drives use System Restore so that space isn't wasted. Select the drive you require and then click on Settings, check the box 'Turn off System Restore on this drive' and click on OK.

You won't be able to use this method to switch System Restore off on your main Windows XP partition, however. To do this, you will have to check the box 'Turn off System Restore on all drives' under the System Restore tab. This should only be done as a last resort, such as if you're running extremely low on disk space.

Restore Location
Any Restore Points that are created either by you or your operating system are stored under C:\System Volume Information. In here is a separate folder for each sub folder, normally kept invisible.

When it comes to using System Restore, you want to be sure that important files aren't lost when you take a step back in time to a Restore Point. Any stored in the My Documents folder should be safe, although files stored elsewhere may not be. To ensure an important folder remains untouched, make an alteration in the Registry and add its location. ■

Keeping up to date

After an operating system is finished and is released in full, the development process still doesn't end. How the latest version is being received by users and the success of its integration with other applications is closely monitored, using feedback gained from the likes of the error reporting process and general support calls.

Microsoft periodically publishes patches and updates that fix problems or secure

security loopholes that have come to light.

As well as this technical side, updates cover upgrades to newer versions of applications such as Internet Explorer. Any updates can be downloaded from **http://windowsupdate.microsoft.com**. Here you will be able to manually select files that you wish to download.

However, following this method involves an element of pot luck. Unless you go to the site every day, you may miss out on a vital update if your visits are infrequent. The best way to keep your operating system up to date is to receive automatic notification from Windows XP.

When you're connected to the Internet, your operating system will check for any relevant updates and notify you via a flashing icon in the system tray. You can alter the way you are informed by clicking on the Automatic Updates tab to configure your Notification Settings. You have three options here. The first is 'Download the updates automatically and notify me when they are ready to be installed'. If you don't mind your bandwidth being tied up, this option is ideal.

A flashing icon will notify you when a download is complete. 'Notify me before downloading any updates and notify me again before installing them on my computer' will tell you that an update is available, again with a flashing icon, leaving you to decide whether or not you want to download it. Finally, 'Turn off automatic updating. I want to update my computer manually' means that you won't receive any notification at all. You'll have to rely on regular visits to the Windows Update site to ensure that you keep abreast of all the current patches and application upgrades.

Remote Assistance

Although available in other applications, this is the first time that a remote assistance utility has been included within a Windows operating system. With this tool, you'll be able to offer or receive direct help rather than using telephone

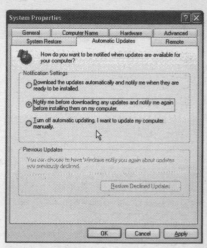

Receive automatic notification that operating system changes are available for your PC

instructions to solve a problem. You'll even be able to connect to PCs running other operating systems, not just Windows XP. Another Windows XP user will be able to connect to your PC too, but you'll need to configure the settings first, under the Remote tab in System Properties.

In order to receive help, make sure that 'Allow Remote Assistance invitations to be sent from this computer' is checked. Then click on the Advanced tab; under Remote Control, 'Allow this computer to be controlled remotely' should be checked.

In order for Remote Assistance to work, both parties connect to the Internet and use either Windows Messenger, Microsoft Outlook or Outlook Express. ■

>> Getting more from Windows Update

When you visit the Windows Update site, you can run a scan of your PC to find out if there are any updates or patches applicable to your system. Once this is done a list of available downloads will be displayed.

■ Critical Updates

Anything that is listed here is vital to the smooth running of your PC, and should always be downloaded and installed. This includes the likes of essential security updates and patches. Installation History:

Clicking on View Installation History is a good way of checking how up to date your PC is. This will list dates and descriptions of downloads you have already made.

■ Windows Update Catalog

If you need a specific update, click on Windows Update Catalog and you'll be able to search for exactly what you need. You may find that this particular link isn't visible on your first visit; if so, click on Personalize Windows Update and check the option to display it.

System Configuration

52 Speed up your system startup

Cut your boot-up time to a minimum with our in-depth guide and advice

54 System configuration utility explained

Seven steps to understanding your PC's system configuration utility

56 Creating your own restore points

If you ever have a problem with Windows XP, you'll need restore points – we have all the info you need

Speed up Startup with the System Configuration Utility

A sluggish startup can be caused by too many applications launching at once. It's quite simple to fix and get your boot-up time down to a minimum – we show you how

When you first bought your Windows XP PC, it probably managed to start itself up in a matter of seconds. However, after you've added countless applications and utilities, the configuration will have changed so much that you may experience delays. The more software applications you install onto your computer the greater the load it places on the available resources, including the processor, operating system, memory and hard drive.

Take a look at your system tray (the area in the bottom right corner by the clock) and you'll see an array of multi coloured

miniature icons. Every item you see here is related to a software application that's configured to start when Windows XP starts. Therefore, along with your operating system you could have at least half a dozen other applications starting up. Although these items are clearly visible there are plenty that aren't and you'll need to delve into your operating system in order to find them.

Windows XP comes with a useful tool that enables you to resolve configuration problems and manage your system's startup process. It's called the System Configuration Utility and you can launch it by clicking on Start > Run and typing msconfig. It's similar

>> Upgraded to Windows XP?

When you upgrade to Windows XP from a previous version of Windows, you may notice that some of your applications no longer launch at startup. This usually affects utilities such as anti-virus programs. They are disabled as a safeguard because some pieces of software can have an effect on the upgrade process. However, it's important to note that after you've installed Windows XP the items that have been disabled automatically will remain so until you decide to reactivate them and start using them again.

To do this, run the System Configuration Utility and ensure that the Startup tab is selected and click on the Restore Startup Programs button. All the applications that have been deactivated will be listed and you'll be able to choose which items you would like to restore to the startup process. Bear in mind that some items may have been disabled because they are not compatible with Windows XP.

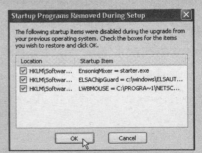

All the startup programs that were removed during upgrade to Windows XP are listed

STEP BY STEP

≫ Removing items from startup

1 LOCATE THE SHORTCUT
Applications that launch when Windows XP boots up aren't always easy to find. There are a number of places where programs can be located. The obvious place is the Startup folder and because of the Windows XP user system there are two of these.

2 DELETE FROM STARTUP FOLDER
The first place is the username\Start Menu\ Programs\Startup folder. Alternatively, it could be in All Users\Start Menu\Programs\Startup. The Registry and Scheduled Tasks folder may also hold shortcut or .exe files.

3 USING MS CONFIG
If you've tried everywhere else then you've no option but to use msconfig. Launch the System Configuration Utility and select the Startup tab. Scroll down the list of programs and then uncheck the item you wish to remove from the Startup process.

to the tool some of you may have used before in Windows 98 and Windows Me and it comes with a few welcome additions in Windows XP. Gone are the tabs for Static VxDs, Environment and International and in come BOOT.INI and Services. Both of these new features can help diagnose any niggles you may be having with starting your PC and will enable you to isolate any processes that may be interfering with your system. In particular, the Services tab contains details of programs that work with other applications and perform specific tasks in Windows XP.

Sorting Startup

To help improve the start times of your PC you'll need to take a look at all the programs that are set to launch automatically when Windows XP boots up.

The applications that are loading can't always be found in the obvious places, so to see which programs are set to run you'll need to take a look at the Startup tab in the System Configuration Utility. A long list of programs here is going to be the main reason why you hear so much crunching and grinding while your PC 'warms up'.

Some of the files you see here are vital to

the running of Windows, while others are related to applications you probably haven't used for some time. A careful check of the list should reveal at least two or three programs that don't actually need to be included in your computer's startup process.

You can prevent applications running automatically by unchecking the box next to a file name. Be careful though, because it's not always clear from the names displayed what a particular item relates to. A curiously named file that you may think is redundant could actually turn out to be your anti-virus program. The best rule of thumb is probably to leave anything you're not sure of.

Proceed with care

Once you've decided on what applications you'd like to leave out of startup, it pays to be cautious and to clear the check boxes one at a time. You can then restart your PC after each one to make sure that the running of your system hasn't been affected in any way. Remember, the System Configuration Utility should only be used as a last resort. You should check individual applications to see if they have a 'launch at startup' option and turn this off within the program itself.

Alternatively, take a look at the Startup folder on the All Programs menu to see if it contains shortcuts to any programs. If there is anything here that you no longer require, just right-click on it and choose Delete.

Program shortcuts can bury themselves deep within Windows, so it pays to use the System Configuration Utility rather than trying to remove them yourself manually.

If you still have problems with a slow startup once you've used the msconfig tool then you'll need to look to other areas of your PC. Doubtless you have plenty of RAM and you'll probably have enough room on your hard drive so it may be worth trying a Registry cleaning utility to clear any redundant entries that may be slowing your system down.

System configuration utility explained

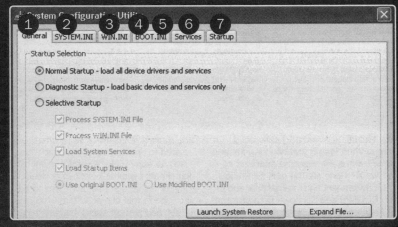

1. General – from here you can select a different startup method to help diagnose problems. Expand file enables you to restore damaged or corrupt system files.

2. System.ini – this contains important driver information and system files. Check or uncheck boxes to select which items you would like to load at startup.

3. Win.ini – details of 16 bit programs that are installed on your PC are stored here, making it easier to track down any applications that are causing you problems.

4. Boot.ini – if you're experiencing problems with startup then it may be necessary to adjust the settings here. This should only be edited by experienced users.

5. See the previous, current, minimum, average and maximum values and how long you've been tracking for.

6. Services – this tab displays a list of programs that work in conjunction with software applications and hardware so they perform correctly.

7 Startup – here you will be able to decide which of your software applications should run automatically when Windows XP boots up. This is also the area where you can reactivate any items that might have been suspended during the upgrade.

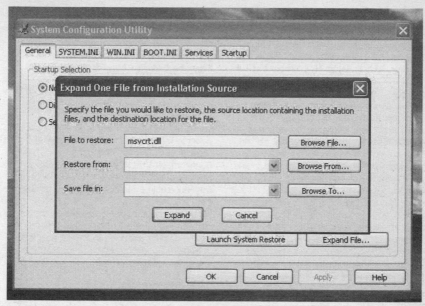

System File Checker has been replaced so you'll need to use Expand File to restore corrupted files

Troubleshooting

We've looked at ways in which you could use the System Configuration Utility to help your PC start up quicker – now we'll focus on how 'msconfig' can assist with diagnosing any system startup problems.

Although having programs starting automatically is supposed to make life easier it can sometimes be more trouble than it's worth. Problems are frequently caused by software conflicts between applications configured to launch at the same time as Windows XP boots up. Using the System Configuration Utility you will be able to alter the settings for the startup process which will in turn help you to diagnose what's causing the trouble.

If all else fails you can always use System Restore under the General tab to put things back to a time when everything worked. However, before making any changes with msconfig.exe it pays to create a restore point yourself.

Should the changes you make in the System Configuration Utility not go according to plan then at least you know you can restore your operating system back to a time when you had a certain level of functionality.

Be selective

If you keep receiving a general error message rather than something specific, try a number of different startup configurations in order to get to the root of the problem.

Launch the System Configuration Utility and select the General tab. Here you will be able to specify exactly which items are loaded. First of all, check Selective Startup and uncheck Load Startup items, click on Apply and restart your PC. This prevents all the applications that normally load from opening automatically when the PC boots.

If this seems to cure things then you know that it's then just a case of going through the items under the Startup tab one at a time until you find the culprit. Alternatively, if they persist then take a closer look at system.ini and win.ini instead. Go through all the command lines in both of these files and look out for any items that are related to the problems you are having and try starting up with them unchecked.

Replace system files

In previous versions of Windows you may have used a useful utility called System File Checker. You could launch this from the Run dialog box and use it to restore vital system files that may have become missing or damaged in some way from your original Windows CD or backup. For those of you who thought 'sfc' had gone forever, don't despair. Click on Expand File and you'll find it here, a slightly cut-down version of its predecessor. It's very straightforward to use, you'll need to enter the name of the file you want to restore.

If it's a damaged file that's still on your system, you can browse to its location.

Next select the location you would like to restore a copy from – this could be your Windows XP CD, floppy disk or hard drive. Under 'Save file in', enter the destination for the replacement file and click OK.

Understanding boot.ini

The options under the boot.ini tab enable you to make changes to the way in which Windows XP boots up. Some of the options can help to speed up the process, for example checking the /NOGUIBOOT box will start windows without any graphical display. However, its main use is to help you diagnose system startup problems. Under [Operating Systems] you will see a line of information for each operating system that appears on your boot menu.

You can verify that the information contained within each one is working correctly by selecting them individually and clicking on Check All Boot Paths. The System Configuration Utility then informs you as to whether or not the lines are OK. Under Boot Options you'll see a list of check boxes and selecting these alters the way in which a particular operating system boots up the next time you restart. The various options can help when you need to try and diagnose a problem. To alter the boot process, tick any of the following boxes:

/SAFEBOOT MINIMAL – Boots the PC in safe mode.

/SAFEBOOT ALTERNATE SHELL – Boots the PC in safe mode, command prompt only.

STEP BY STEP

>> How to create your own restore points

Use Restore Points to 'undo' changes you've made that might have caused problems

1 INSTALLING NEW SOFTWARE
If you're going to make changes to your system by installing new software or adding new hardware then System Restore can take a snapshot of your system. Should you run into problems, you can go back to a point when everything worked OK.

2 CREATE A RESTORE POINT USING SYSTEM RESTORE
To make a restore point, or 'system checkpoint' as they are called, click on Start, All Programs, Accessories, System Tools and choose System Restore. Select Create a restore point and then simply click Next.

3 USING F8 DURING START-UP
If your system fails completely, press F8 during startup and restore from the last good configuration. Alteratively, if you can get into Windows, go to System Restore and choose 'Restore my computer to an earlier time' and choose your restore point.

❯❯ Putting safe mode on the menu

It doesn't take long to create a Safe Mode in case something goes wrong

Instead of pressing F8 to access safe mode you can add an option for it to your operating system boot menu. Right-click on My Computer and choose Properties, then select the Advanced tab and click on Startup and Recovery. Click on Settings and then under System startup click on Edit to launch a copy of your boot.ini file in notepad. Under [Operating Systems], highlight the line of your default operating system, right-click on it and choose Copy, then paste it at the bottom of the list. At the end of the line copy the following:
/safeboot:minimal /sos /bootlog

Change the description from "Microsoft Windows XP Home Edition" to read something like "Windows XP Home Edition Safe Mode". Then close the file saving the changes you have made. The next time you restart your PC you'll have an additional option on the menu, enabling you to start in safe mode.

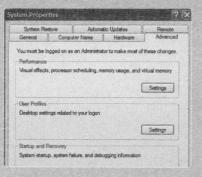

/NOGUIBOOT – This starts Windows XP without any graphical display.

/BOOTLOG – Creates a bootlog – a file containing details of what happens when starting up.

/BASEVIDEO – Boots the PC using the standard VGA driver, ideal for dealing with video card problems.

/SOS – Displays the names of drivers as they load up.

Managing Services

The only area of the System Configuration Utility we haven't looked at yet is the Services tab. These are processes that work in conjunction with certain programs and applications. For example, click on the tab and take look at the list of processes and you'll see the likes of Windows audio, Plug and Play and Windows installer.

Some of these are vital to the running of your operating system while others don't have as much significance. When you select Diagnostic startup from the General tab most of these Services will be disabled and only the bare minimum necessary for running Windows XP will be started.

As part of the diagnosis for a system problem you can disable control Services

manually by unchecking the box next to a particular item. However, before you start doing this, make sure you check the box 'Hide All Microsoft Services'.

By doing this any important Windows XP services will be removed from view so there's no chance of you stopping anything that's needed for the safe running of the operating system.

Management of your PC's services can also help to speed things up on your PC as each process will be adding to the load that your CPU has to deal with. Scroll down the list and look out for any processes which you think you don't currently need. The System Config Utility will be able to help with the service management.

For more control over background tasks it's best to use the Task Manager. ■

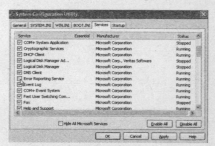

Using msconfig.exe is the safest way to make changes

Registry tweaks and tricks

60 Backing up the Registry

How to tweak safe in the knowledge that you have a full back-up of your Registry

67 Enhanced online experience

Use the Registry to alter email settings, speed up net access, protect your browser and more!

71 Extra privacy and security

Change Internet Explorer to keep all of your online activity private

Tweaking the Registry

In this chapter, we take an in-depth look at the Registry and explain how you can enhance Windows XP by making a few simple changes

Y ou've probably heard talk of the Windows Registry before and how you should avoid it like the plague unless you're an advanced PC user. While it's true that changing the wrong line of code can cause your system terminal damage, it isn't all bad news. For those with a little PC knowledge – and the right instructions – editing the Registry can actually enhance your PC.

Your operating system comes with its own tool for editing this aspect of your system, called the Registry Editor. To launch it, click on Start then Run, type regedit and

click on Enter. You'll see what looks like a selection of folders. Don't be deceived. The Registry is actually made up of two hidden system files that are located in your Windows folder. They're called USER.DAT and SYSTEM.DAT and it's only possible to access their contents by using the Registry Editor. The folders and sub folders you can see in the left pane are referred to as Keys and Sub keys respectively. In the right pane, you'll see their associated values. These system files hold all the information about the hardware and software that's installed on your PC. In particular, the Registry

>> Backing up the Registry

System Restore is just one way to keep your system fault-free while you tweak...

Rather than using System Restore and replacing the Registry in its entirety, why not simply back up the section you'll be working on instead? Should your changes not work as expected, you can just merge your backup file and the alterations you've made are cancelled out automatically.

To back up part of the Registry, make sure that the Key you want to preserve is selected in the left-hand pane. Click on File > Export and choose a location for the file you want to save. You can choose from four different file formats, but we would recommend that you use the Registry Hive Files format when making a selective backup. If you need to Restore using your Hive file, then select the same Key in the Registry, choose the Import option from the File menu and locate your backup. You'll then be prompted for your confirmation that the Key and Sub keys are about to be overwritten.

STEP BY STEP

>> Speeding up the Start Menu

1 A QUESTION OF SPEED
While you've been using Windows XP you've probably noticed the delay in the Start Menu appearing after you've clicked on the Start button. By editing the Registry, you can adjust this time delay and make the menu pop up faster or slower.

2 DELAY CONFIGURATION
Open the Registry Editor by clicking on Start > Run, then type regedit and click on OK. Locate the following key HKEY_ CURRENT_USER\Control Panel\Desktop. Now, in the right pane, scroll down to MenuShowDelay, right-click on it and choose Modify.

3 THE NUMBER GAME
The amount in the Value data field will read 400. To speed up the rate at which the Start Menu displays, you need to reduce this figure. Dropping it to 200 gives a noticeable improvement. Reduce it further if you're keen to see it pop up even faster.

---

contains configurations details such as user profiles and hardware preferences vital to Windows XP.

Restore the Registry

As a safeguard, you should always back up all or part of your Registry before editing it. System Restore is one way of doing this. Should you run into problems after you've made changes to Windows XP or the Registry, you always know a working copy is available at restart.

Before making any changes, it's also a good idea to set restore points manually. Using Restore itself is pretty straightforward: restart your PC and while it's restarting keep pressing the F8 key. Instead of the Windows Start Up Menu of previous versions, you'll see the 'Windows Advanced Options Menu'. Using the arrow keys, go up to 'Last Known Good Configuration (your most recent settings that worked)' to highlight it and press Enter to initiate the process.

New right-click option

This is a slight adjustment to Windows Explorer that enables you to explore the contents of a particular folder without displaying all other folders as well. Locate HKEY_CLASSES_ROOT\Folder\Shell. Right-click on Shell, choose New > Key and call it Explore folder. Right-click on this, create another new Key and call it command.

Make sure that command is highlighted, then in the right pane, right-click on (Default) and choose Modify. Under value data, type explorer.exe /e,/root,%1, then click on OK. Now right-click on any folder to see the new menu option.

Sort Start Menu

When you install software applications in Windows XP, they aren't added to the Start menu in any particular order. Normally, the only way to sort them is to right-click the menu and then arrange them alphabetically. This simple Registry tweak, however, gets Windows XP to do this for you automatically. Use regedit to find HKEY_CURRENTUSER\ Software\Microsoft\Windows\CurrentVersion \Explorer\MenuOrder\StartMenu\ &Programs\Menu.

In the right pane will be a Key called Order. Right-click on this and choose Delete. Restart Windows and your Start menu is now sorted alphabetically.

Remove balloon tips

While the pop-up balloon tips in Windows XP are useful and informative to newcomers, more experienced users will be pleased to hear that you can turn them off with just a tweak of the Registry.

First, find this Key HKEY_CURRENT_USER\Software\Microsoft\Windows\Current Version\Explorer\Advanced. Right-click on Advanced and choose New> DWORD Value and label it EnableBalloonTips. Now right-click on it, choose Modify and amend the Value data to 0. (0 disables the balloon tips; 1 re-enables them.)

Refine Start Menu

This Registry change refines the Start Menu so that it only displays items you need. Go to this Key HKEY_CURRENT_USER\Software\Microsoft\Windows\CurrentVersion\Policies\Explorer, then right-click on Explorer and choose New > DWORD Value. Call it NoSMMyDocs then right-click on it, select Modify and give it a value of 1. (1 deletes the folder; 0 displays it.)

My Computer

Want to restrict the information displayed in My Computer to details of your drives only and remove all references to shared folders?

Then read on. Using the Registry Editor, go along to HKEY_LOCAL_MACHINE\Software\Microsoft\Windows\CurrentVersion\Explorer\MyComputer\NameSpace\DelegateFolders. Here you'll see a key named {59031a47-3f72-44a7-89c5-5595fe6b30ee}. Right-click on this and choose Delete. Close the Registry Editor, then restart Windows XP and go into My Computer to see the results.

Add system shortcuts

For useful shortcuts to your Start Menu, try the following. Locate this Key HKEY_CLASSES_ROOT\CLSID and you'll see a long list of folders. Each one represents an item such as Control Panel, Printers or Inbox. In order to create a shortcut to Control Panel items on your Start Menu, create a new folder on your desktop and name it Control Panel.{21EC20 20 -3AEA-1069-A2DD-08002B30309D}.

You can now place this icon wherever you like and use it as a shortcut. Other examples include Printers.{2227A280-3AEA-1069-A2DE-08002B30309D} and Network Neighbourhood.{208D2C60-3AEA-1069-A2D7-08002B30309D}.

For some more examples, simply take a look in the folders which can be found in HKEY_CLASSES_ROOT\CLSID.

⟩⟩ Your Registry explained

Here's our quick guide to what's in the Registry and what it's for

HKEY_CLASSES_ROOT This section of the Registry maintains information relating to program shortcuts. When a file is double-clicked, this part of the Registry tells Windows XP which program to open.

HKEY_CURRENT_USER Configuration information for individual users is stored here. For example, the way a person has set their folder options, screen savers, colour settings and Control Panel options.

HKEY_LOCAL_MACHINE Details of all the hardware that's installed on your PC, together with any software applications, is stored here. This information remains the same and does not change for individual users.

HKEY_USERS This is the part of the Registry where details of the user profiles that have been set up are

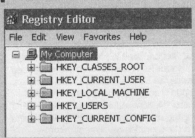

stored. **HKEY_CURRENT_USER** is a Sub key of this and stores the individual settings.

HKEY_CURRENT_CONFIG You may have set up different hardware profiles in Windows XP. When you start Windows XP, details of the hardware configuration that is to be used is stored here.

>> How to quickly restart the registry

Don't reboot, try this instead

After you've spent some time making alterations and modifications within the registry, you'll soon notice that there's a slight drawback with the whole process – you need to restart your PC every time in order for your changes to take effect. As you'll no doubt discover very rapidly, this can start to get rather tiresome after a couple of alterations.

Fortunately, there's a simple trick which you can perform that will solve this very problem and will reset your Registry without you having to wait for your PC to restart every time you make a change.

All you have to do is press Ctrl+Alt+Delete to open Windows Task Manager and click on the processes tab. Your next step is to simply scroll down the list, highlight explorer.exe and click on End Process. Once you've done this, click on File, New, enter Explorer and click on OK to restart your Registry.

Image Name	User Name	CPU	Mem Usage
ePrompter.exe	USER	00	5,544 K
ctfmon.exe	USER	00	2,192 K
avgcc32.exe	USER	00	1,256 K
DAP.exe	USER	00	6,652 K
qttask.exe	USER	00	760 K
svchost.exe	SYSTEM	00	2,300 K
explorer.exe	USER	02	29,564 K
nvsvc32.exe	SYSTEM	00	956 K
avgserv.exe	SYSTEM	00	1,248 K
taskmgr.exe	USER	02	3,908 K
spoolsv.exe	SYSTEM	00	3,868 K
svchost.exe	LOCAL SERVICE	00	3,000 K
svchost.exe	NETWORK SERVICE	00	2,692 K

Fix-its and tricks

There may come a time when you need to go into the Registry to remove any redundant entries relating to a program that has been uninstalled. Unless you know the specific location of the Key or sub key you need to edit you'll find the Registry a difficult place to navigate.

Although there is consistency in the way it is laid out it's not always obvious where you will find certain items. If you are looking for something specific, such as elements of a software application, then the best method is to use the Registry Editor's Find tool.

Open the Registry Editor and click on Edit, Find, enter your search criteria then press Enter to begin your search. A search will begin and anything found matching your criteria will be highlighted. After you've edited that item, or if you want to continue searching, there's no need to click on Edit, Find again. Just press F3 and the Find tool will carry on from where it left off, and having remembered your criteria will search for the next occurrence. Keep pressing F3 to search until a full scan has been completed.

If you return frequently to any particular areas of the Registry you can do so more quickly by bookmarking the Key or sub key. Highlight the one you wish to work on then click on Favorites, Add to Favorites. You can then return to your preferred areas in the

same way you do in Internet Explorer. As the Registry is such a vital part of the operating system, you should back up before making any changes. At the very minimum you should back up the Key or sub key you plan to work on.

A problem solved

No doubt there have been times when you have eagerly installed an item of freeware or shareware onto your PC only to find later that the uninstall facility doesn't work.

Having gone into Windows Explorer and deleted all the related files and folders manually you're still left with an annoying entry in your Add/Remove Programs list.

This information is stored in the Windows XP Registry so the only way to remove it is to use the Registry Editor. The actual information relating to the Add/Remove Programs entries can be found at HKEY_LOCAL_MACHINE/
Software/Microsoft/Windows/CurrentVersion/Uninstall. Click on the + symbol to expand the key and reveal all the sub keys. Scroll down the list until you see a sub key that matches the program name that you want to remove.

Once you've located it, just right-click and Delete. Open the Add/Remove Programs tool and you'll see that all trace of your program has been removed.

You can clean the Registry by hand, but it's advisable to use a program such as Registry Healer or McAfee Registry Wizard.

Before and after

Having made changes to your Registry by editing Keys or installing new applications you may wish to view your alterations. The easiest way is to Export your Registry as a text file before you make the changes and then do the same again afterwards. You'll then be able to use the file checking tool FC.EXE to compare both files. Click on Start, Run, type command and press Enter. At the prompt type the following, 'fc /u before.txt after.txt > compare.txt'. The file compare.txt is where the results of the FC.EXE comparison will be saved.

Changing the interface

The new look interface offered by Windows XP is impressive, but if you're suffering from pangs of nostalgia then you can make the operating system display the old look menu by adding a line to the Registry. Locate HKEY_CURRENT_USER \Software\ Microsoft\Windows\CurrentVersion\Policies \Explorer then, in the left pane, right-click on

Explorer and select New, DWORD Value. Call it NoSimpleStartMenu then right-click on it, choose Modify and give it a Value of 1 to make it use the classic style menu. A value of 0 will ensure that the default Windows XP look is used.

Restrict users' access

You can discourage users from making alterations to the Start Menu by editing the Registry. This slight alteration will prevent them from being able to right click on the menu and modify it. Make sure that you are logged in as the user whose access you want to restrict then find this key: HKEY_CURRENT_USER\ Software\ Microsoft\Windows\CurrentVersion\Policies\ Explorer. Right-click on Explorer in the left pane and choose New, DWORD Value and name it NoChangeStartMenu. Then right-click on it, choose Modify and give it a value of 1 to bring the restriction into effect. Alternatively, to allow access again, change this value to 0.

Customise My Computer

Restrict the information displayed in My Computer to details of your drives only and

---

STEP BY STEP

≫ Importing .REG files safely

Double click a .REG file by mistake and you'll import it to the Registry

1 **EDIT NOT IMPORT**
When you double-click on a .REG file, that file will be imported straight into your Registry. You can avoid importing this kind of file by mistake by configuring a double-click on such a file to open Notepad instead.

2 **FIND THE KEY**
Click on Start, Run, type regedit and click on OK to launch the Registry Editor. Locate this key: HKEY_CLASSES_ROOT\regfile \shell. In the right pane, right-click on Default and choose Modify.

3 **MERGE IF NECESSARY**
Then under Value data you need to enter the word 'edit'. When you next double-click on a .REG file a notepad Window will open instead. If you need to import a .REG file just right-click on it and choose Merge.

>>COMMON SUB KEY NAMES

If you're working in the Registry, it's useful to know a few sub key names

Administrative Tools	{D20EA4E1-3957-11d2-A40B-0C5020524153}
Briefcase	{85BBD920-42A0-1069-A2E4-08002B30309D}
Control Panel	{21EC2020-3AEA-1069-A2DD-08002b30309d}
Fonts	{D20EA4E1-3957-11d2-A40B-0C5020524152}
History	{FF393560-C2A7-11CF-BFF4-444553540000}
Microsoft Network	{00028B00-0000-0000-C000-000000000046}
My Computer	{20D04FE0-3AEA-1069-A2D8-08002B30309D}
My Documents	{450D8FBA-AD25-11D0-98A8-0800361B1103}
Printers and Faxes	{2227A280-3AEA-1069-A2DE-08002B30309D}
Programs Folder	{7be9d83c-a729-4d97-b5a7-1b7313c39e0a}
Recycle Bin	{645FF040-5081-101B-9F08-00AA002F954E}
Scanners and Cameras	{E211B736-43FD-11D1-9EFB-0000F8757FCD}
Scheduled Tasks	{D6277990-4C6A-11CF-8D87-00AA0060F5BF}
Start Menu Folder	{48e7caab-b918-4e58-a94d-505519c795dc}
Temporary Internet Files	{7BD29E00-76C1-11CF-9DD0-00A0C9034933}
Web Folders	{BDEADF00-C265-11d0-BCED-00A0C90AB50F}

remove all references to shared folders. Using the Registry Editor go along to HKEY_LOCAL_MACHINE\ Software\Microsoft \Windows\CurrentVersion\Explorer\ MyComputer\NameSpace\ DelegateFolders. Here you will see a key {59031a47-3f72-44a7-89c5-5595fe6b30e}. Right-click on this and choose Delete. Close the Registry Editor then restart Windows XP and go into My Computer to see the results.

Open with... more programs

Right-click on any file and you can select 'Open with' and choose which program you would like to use to open that file. You can add an application that's not listed by going along to HKEY_CURRENT_USER\Software \Microsoft\Windows\CurrentVersion\Explore r\FileExts. Each file extension is represented by a key. Select the one you want to amend and add the program you want to use to the OpenWithList sub key.

Lock Taskbar

It can be extremely annoying when you return to your PC after someone else has been using it and they've altered your desktop settings in some way, in particular the location of the Taskbar. This Registry tweak enables you to lock it down and stop it being moved by other users. Locate this key

HKEY_CURRENT_USER\Software\Microsoft\ Windows\CurrentVersion\Policies \Explorer. In the left pane right click on Explorer and create a new DWORD value and call it LockTaskbar. To lock the Taskbar give it a value of 0, or 1 if you wish to unlock it.

Keeping it private

You may not want other people to see the files you have been looking at on your PC. To stop prying eyes you can make sure that the recent documents list on the Start menu is cleared each time you reboot or log off Windows. You can do this by going to: HKEY_CURRENT_USER\Software\Microsoft\ Windows\CurrentVersion\Policies\ Explorer. Right-click on Explorer, create a new DWORD value and call it ClearRecentDocsOnExit. You then need to enter a value. 0 disables the feature while 1 will enable it.

Control desktop icons

You may not want items such as My Computer to be visible. This adjustment enables you to remove them from view, or you can use a variation to add certain tools to the desktop that are usually tucked away. For example, you can add an icon for the likes of the Control Panel, History and Programs folders. To delete an icon, you need to locate this key:

HKEY_LOCAL_MACHINE\ software\Microsoft \Windows\CurrentVersion\Explorer\ Desktop \NameSpace.

Browse through all the sub keys, and for any that you don't need, just right-click and choose Delete. If the icon doesn't disappear from your desktop immediately then hit F5 to refresh the display.

Add right-click options

When you're working with folders and right-click the mouse there are a range of useful options that appear. However, you can add two new options to the right-click menu by first locating this key: HKEY_CLASSES_ ROOT\ Directory\shellex\ ContextMenuHandlers. Right-click on ContextMenuHandlers in the left pane and choose New, Key.

Call it 'Copy to' and then in the right pane right-click on (Default), choose Modify and give it the value {C2FBB630-2971-11d1- A18C-00C04FD75D13}.

To add a 'Move to Folder' option, simply repeat the process but this time make sure you call the key 'Move to' and give it a value {C2FBB631-2971-11d1-A18C- 00C04FD75D13}.

Add version number

Anyone who tried the beta version of Windows XP will remember that the operating version number was displayed in the bottom right corner of the desktop. You can restore this to view by changing one simple setting. System administrators or PC technicians may find this tip particularly useful. Find the key: HKEY_CURRENT_USER\ Control Panel\Desktop then right-click on PaintDesktopVersion and choose Modify. Enter a value of 1 to display the version or 0 to disable it.

Disable CD burning

Windows XP makes it easy to burn CDs it's just a case of dragging and dropping files onto your CDR or CDRW to copy them. However, this Registry tweak will give you control over this and will enable you to disable the feature. Go to this location in the Registry: HKEY_CURRENT_USER\Software\ Microsoft\Windows\CurrentVersion\Policies\ Explorer. In the pane on the left-hand side, right-click on Explorer and choose New, DWORD Value and call it NoCDBurning. Then simply right-click on it and give it a value of 1 to disable CD burning or 0 to enable it.

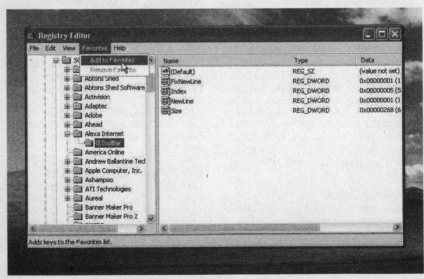

You can add keys or sub keys that you use frequently to a Favorites list

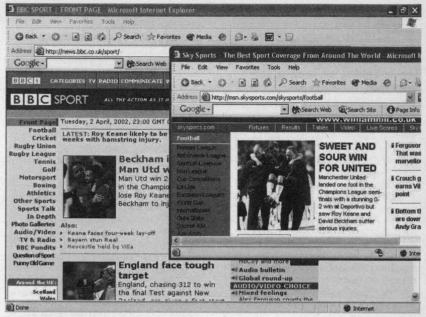

Use the Registry to stop browser windows appearing off screen and out of view

Maximum power!

Now we're going to turn our attention to your Internet connection and applications. When most new PCs are shipped, Windows XP is configured to run with settings that ensure stability and reliability. However, there's nothing to stop you changing these settings to get the best performance and efficiency for your set up. The time will come when you want to personalise things, especially when using the Internet.

There are a number of settings you can alter within Windows XP that will improve performance without the need to upgrade hardware. Delve into the Registry and you'll discover a number of ways to improve your connection, browser and email programs.

Speed boosters

When it comes to making your internet connection faster, you may have seen the myriad of so called Internet boosters and accelerators on offer. Although they seem to

perform mysterious high tech shenanigans to increase your speed, all they're actually doing is tweaking a few Registry settings.

So put your credit card away: there's no need to go off and purchase additional software. We'll show you all you need to know about making these changes to the Windows XP Registry yourself.

Browser protection

Web sites are able to gather information about you via your browser. In the main this

Expert Tip

■ A larger Receive Window will benefit high bandwidth connections. By reducing the size of the Window, on the other hand, an acknowledgement will be sent to the sender that data has been received. This can help to stop time outs on your connection.

is done by cookies whose information is constantly updated. You may also have noticed some increasingly aggressive marketing tactics while browsing the Web. Certain sites use a method where they can alter the URL you use for your browser's home page, so that it displays their home page or product each time you launch your web browser.

Another tactic is for a Web site to fill your screen with a browser window, forcing you to see the details of a product or service. We'll show you how to stop your browser windows being manipulated by intrusive Web sites. There are other security and privacy considerations as well. Internet Explorer can memorise all your previous browser activity and recall it for you. Those who would rather not have this kind of information recorded can opt to remove it via the Registry.

There are other ways in which you can customise Internet Explorer, both aesthetically and to help you work more efficiently. These include the addition and removal of menu items, along with changes to various notification boxes.

Email alterations

Anyone who uses Microsoft Outlook 2002 will notice the security feature that prevents the opening and saving of potentially dangerous file attachments. Around 30 file types are restricted, including .exe, .bat and .vbs files. There may be occasions when you need to access such attachments and know they are safe. Normally there would be no simple way of doing this, as the option can't be disabled within Outlook. A change to the Registry will enable you to freely open and use these files.

There's also a selection of Registry alterations for Outlook Express, including a security feature that prevents the alteration of any mail or news accounts.

Speed up your Internet connection

You don't need to invest in extra software when you can make performance enhancements yourself – changing just three settings can have a positive effect.

The MTU setting (Maximum Transmission Unit) is the packet size limit for data that you send out from your PC to pass through your ISP. You can find out your ISP's MTU by opening a command prompt window and typing 'ping -f -l [packet size] www.[your ISP].com'.

Use a packet size value between 0 and 1500; most ISPs' limit is 576, so this is a

---

STEP BY STEP

>> Boosting your internet connection

Three straightforward Registry changes to make your net access faster

1 ADJUST MTU
After determining your MTU by pinging your ISP, you can add this value to your Registry. Go to HKEY_LOCAL_MACHINE\ System\CurrentControlSet\ Services\Class\NetTrans. In the right pane you'll see MaxMTU; right click on this to modify it and add your new value.

2 ADJUST MSS
Go to HKEY_LOCAL_ MACHINE\System\ CurrentControlSet\ Services\Class\NetTrans. In the right pane right click on DefaultMSS, choose Modify and add a new value. The figure you enter should be around 30 less than the MTU value you've already entered.

3 ADJUST RECEIVE WINDOW
The Receive Window should be an even multiple of the TCP Maximum Segment Size (MSS). Locate the key HKEY_LOCAL_ MACHINE\SYSTEM\ CurrentControlSet\Services\ Tcpip\Parameters, and in the right pane change the TCPWindowSize to 64240.

Find out your ISP's MTU size using a command line ping

good place to start. Keep raising the figure until you're told the packet was fragmented. The highest figure you obtained before this error is the MTU.

The MSS (Maximum Segment Size) limits the amount of data that can be put into a packet; this value is smaller than the Maximum Transmission Unit. The TTL (Time to Live) setting decides how many times a data packet should try to find its destination before giving up.

Finally, the Receive Window setting decides how much data your PC can receive. It's important to get this right, because a figure that's too high or low can result in packet loss or slowness.

Download location

If you use Windows XP as your download manager, the Registry controls the directory where all your files are saved.

To change the folder, locate the HKEY_CURRENT_USER\.DEFAULT\Software\ Microsoft\Internet Explorer key. In the right pane, right click on Download Directory and choose Modify. Now, under 'Value data', change the directory.

Software updates

Your browser will try to update automatically from time to time. You can turn this feature off if you prefer. Go to HKEY_CURRENT_ USER\Software\Microsoft\Internet Explorer\Main; in the right pane, locate NoUpdateCheck.

It will currently have a value of 1; you should right click and change this to 0 to disable the function.

Jargon

■ Hexadecimal

Some entries in the Registry seem to use a combination of letters and numbers, but they're actually numerical values described using the hexadecimal system. Our standard decimal system uses ten values, from 0 to 9; the hexadecimal system uses 16 values, going from 0 to 9 then adding A, B, C, D, E and F. So 10 in decimal is shown in hexadecimal as 'A', 15 is shown as 'F' and 16 is shown as '10'.

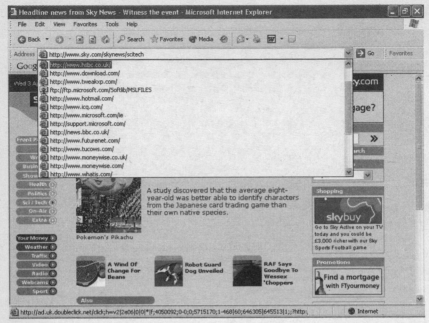

You can keep your browsing habits private from anyone else that shares your PC

Remove links folder

Look in your Favorites list and you'll see a folder called Links. You can right click and delete it, but it's recreated when you restart your PC. To remove it permanently, go to HKEY_CURRENT_USER\Software\Microsoft\ Internet Explorer\Toolbar, then right click on LinksFolderName. Choose Modify and delete the entry in 'Value data'. Now open Internet Explorer and delete the Links folder.

Amend AutoComplete

The AutoComplete feature will finish off words as you type, along with giving you the option to choose a word from a drop down list. This Registry edit can alter the feature so only the drop down box appears. Locate HKEY_CURRENT_USER\Software\Microsoft\ Windows\CurrentVersion\Explorer\AutoCom plete, then edit the Append Completion value to read 'no'.

Line up windows

Browser windows can be located partially off

screen sometimes, making it difficult to close or minimise them. To keep Internet Explorer in its rightful position, find the Key HKEY_CURRENT_USER\Software\Microsoft\ Internet Explorer\Main. In the right pane you will see a value called Window Placement: right click it and choose Delete. Your alignment problems are solved.

Enhancing your Internet security

Automatic home page resetting is one of the most intrusive things that can happen to you on the Web. However, the Registry can prevent much extraneous manipulation. Make sure that your home page is displaying the URL you want to keep, then locate HKEY_USERS\.DEFAULT\Software\Policies\ Microsoft\Internet Explorer. Right click on Internet Explorer and create a Sub Key called ControlPanel, then a DWORD value called Homepage. Right click on ControlPanel, select Modify and give it a value of 1 in order to protect your home page.

Control windows

This Registry alteration lets you minimise new browser windows into the taskbar.

There are two settings to adjust, depending on how you want new windows to appear. The first controls the way in which a new window appears. Go to HKEY_CURRENT _USER\ControlPanel\Desktop and create a DWORD called ForegroundLockTimeout, or modify the existing one. The value you give it will determine how long a new window takes to appear over the old one. Enter a value of 0 and the new window will go over the top immediately. Enter the default value of 200000 (0x00030d40 hexadecimal): the new window will appear on top for 200,000 milliseconds and then minimise to the taskbar, where it will flash.

This behaviour is controlled by the next tweak, which will set the number of flashes. Create or modify the DWORD value ForegroundFlashCount, and set a value for the number of flashes you require. 0 will make it flash infinitely or you can go for the default value of 3.

Blocked attachments

It's impossible to open certain file types in Outlook 2002 if they're attached to an email. The only way around this is togo to HKEY_CURRENT_USER\Software\Microsoft \Office\10.0\Outlook\Security. In the right pane, right click and create a new string value called Level1Remove. The values for this item are any file types that you would like to unblock, each separated by a semi colon. For example, entering 'exe;bat' would unblock .exe executable and .bat batch files.

Express splash

Whenever you open Outlook Express, a window appears on screen showing the program name; this is called the splash screen. It can delay the opening of the program when all you want to do is to check your email messages. To remove it, go to HKEY_CURRENT_USER\Identities\[Your Identity]\Software\Microsoft\Outlook Express\5.0 and create a new DWORD value and give it a value of 1. Start Outlook Express and no more splash screen! ∎

STEP BY STEP

≫ Maintaining Privacy and Security

Change the way Internet Explorer works for a better sense of security

1 EDIT YOUR HISTORY
One of the problems of using a shared PC is that your online activity is going to be visible to the next person to use the machine. To clear individual URLs from the History, go to HKEY_CURRENT _USER\Software\Microsoft\ Internet Explorer\TypedURLs. Right click on any URL you want to conceal and then choose Delete.

2 BLOCK FILE ACCESS IN IE
The address bar in Internet Explorer can give you access to files on your hard drive as well as Internet URLs. To turn this feature off, go to HKEY_LOCAL_ MACHINE\Software\Microsoft\ Windows\CurrentVersion\ Policies and create a new Key called Explorer. Give it a new DWORD value called NoFileURL with a value of 1.

3 BAR AUTOMATIC INSTALLS
This adjustment stops the likes of Comet Cursor from installing. Go to HKEY_LOCAL_MACHINE\ SOFTWARE\Microsoft\ Windows\CurrentVersion\ Internet Settings\ZoneMap\ Domains. Create a Sub Key named after the site you want to block. Give the Sub Key a DWORD value called * and set its value to 4.

Enhanced Privacy

74 Convert your file system to NTFS

Providing multiple users with secure disk partitions ensures their privacy

75 Using Cacls to secure a file

Users of Windows XP Home Edition can use Cacls to restrict access to certain files

77 Protecting yourself while on the internet

Practical advice for dealing with cookies and web bugs to ensure your privacy

Enhanced privacy

Convert your file system to NTFS and reap the rewards. We show you how to implement the enhanced security features of Windows XP...

With previous versions of Windows, it's always been possible to set up individual user logins and regulate access to certain parts of the operating system. This process only really controlled display and Internet settings, though. In order to stop other areas of the system being tampered with, it would've been necessary to try and master the policy editor, something an inexperienced PC user probably wouldn't have wanted to tackle.

Today, with the shared PC becoming more commonplace in households

everywhere, it's possible to keep one individual's work completely separate from another, thanks to Windows XP. And there's a great deal more to privacy and security in Windows XP than just individual logins.

We'll explore in detail what Windows XP can offer to ensure your files, folders and personal information stay secure from other people that use your PC and during the time you spend online.

Back to basics

The file system that you're running on a particular hard drive partition will determine

>> Backing up the Registry

System Restore is just one way to keep your system fault-free while you tweak...

Rather than using System Restore and replacing the Registry in its entirety, why not simply back up the section you'll be working on instead? Should your changes not work as expected, you can just merge your backup file and the alterations you've made are cancelled out automatically.

To back up part of the Registry, make sure that the Key you want to preserve is selected in the left-hand pane. Click on File > Export and choose a location for the file you want to save. You can choose from four different file formats, but we would recommend that you use the Registry Hive Files format when making a selective backup. If you need to Restore using your Hive file, then select the same Key in the Registry, choose the Import option from the File menu and locate your backup. You'll then be prompted for your confirmation that the Key and Sub keys are about to be overwritten.

>> Using Cacls to secure a file

1 VIEW PERMISSIONS
To use Cacls to view what permissions have been set for a particular file, first open a command prompt window. At the prompt, type cacls, followed by the full document path. For example, cacls c:\data\newsletter.doc. Press Enter to disply the permissions

2 UNDERSTANDING PERMISSIONS
Next to each user account on your PC will be a single letter. This letter describes the level of access that a user has over that file. There are three permission settings available, as follows: F is Full access, C is Change and R is Read only.

3 SETTING PERMISSIONS
By adding switches and changing command line parameters, you can easily change the level of access a user has to a particular file or folder. To illustrate: David requires Full access to a folder, while Peter requires Read only – thus, cacls c:\data /g david:f peter:r

how much security you can place over the files and folders on your PC. For example, to have the full range of security options available at your disposal, a partition will have to be formatted as NTFS rather than FAT or FAT32. The advantages of NTFS are that it's more secure and reliable than its rivals. It's better at tracking disk activity and recovering from errors. Windows XP comes with its own tool, Convert, for converting FAT drives to NTFS. You'll be glad to hear that the process won't result in the loss of any data as would have been the case if you'd opted for FDISK, so there's no need to buy third-party partition management software.

Warning!

Before you rush off to convert your existing

Compress a folder, then give it a password to ensure that its contents stay safe

FAT or FAT 32 partition to NTFS, though, a word of warning. NTFS will not work with Windows 95, 98 or Me as none of them will recognise it.

Therefore, if you have a multiboot PC that uses one of these operating systems along with Windows XP, all on the same partition, you'll need to ensure that the partition is set up as FAT32. Furthermore, once you've converted a drive from FAT32 to NTFS, there's no going back. The only way to

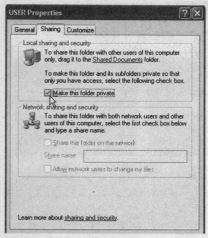

Hide your My Documents folder from other users

reverse the process is to use the FDISK utility which results in the loss of all the data on that partition.

File compression

Having converted your partition to NTFS, one of the new features you can take advantage of is file and folder compression. Once your data is compressed, you can add a password and restrict access to it.

To create a zipped compressed folder (archive) open Windows Explorer and highlight the folder you wish to archive. Right-click on it and select Send To > Compressed (zipped) Folder. A file is then created with the zip file extension.

In order to password-protect the contents of this file, double-click on it to display its

contents, then click on File > Add Password. Enter a password and confirm it.

Protect your profile

During the setup of Windows XP (if you had an NTFS partition), you'd have been given the option to make the files and folders of your user account private, thus preventing other users from accessing them as well.

If you didn't select this option initially you can invoke it now and hide your My Documents folder so that any other users that log on to the same PC won't be able to see it. To do this, click on Start > Run, type %systemdrive%\ documents and settings and click on OK. Then open My Computer, locate the Documents and Settings folder and right-click on it. Choose Sharing and Security from the menu and place a tick in the box labelled 'Make this folder private'. Click on OK to apply these changes.

The next time another user logs on to the PC, they'll no longer be able to see your My Document folder. Better still, any user that double-clicks on your profile icon in Documents and Settings will receive an 'access denied' message.

Set NTFS Permissions

For users of Windows XP Home Edition, the range of file sharing access levels aren't quite as wide as those found in Windows XP Professional Edition. However, there is a utility that gives them back some control. Called Cacls, it can be used to view and set permissions for any file or folder on your system. See the previous page for instructions on how to use it and below for a list of parameters.

>>CACLS COMMAND LINE SWITCHES

Configure Cacls using the following easy-to-remember command line switches

/T	Change permissions of a file in a directory and all subdirectories
/E	Edits access control list rather than replacing it
/C	Lets a user continue when an 'access denied' error appears
/G user:permissions	Gives a user the specified access rights – this replaces existing permissions unless used with /E
/R user	Use with /E to remove a user's access rights
/P user:permissions	Use this to replace a user's access rights
/D user	Stops a particular user accessing a file or folder

Privacy and security

Although there are many safeguards in place, the internet is still not fully secure. However, there's no need to start panicking and pulling the modem connection from the phone socket, it's really not as bad as all that. If you're in possession of the facts then you're in a better position to deal effectively with security while you're online.

When you connect to the internet you are a potential target for two groups of people, criminals and marketing organisations. The former may try to obtain personal information from your computer such as credit card or bank account details that will then be used for fraudulent purposes.

One way this can be achieved is by infecting your PC with a certain type of virus that is configured to relay your personal data back to the perpetrator of the infection. Alternatively, they may try and hack directly into your internet connection via any weakness they can find at your ISP or with any software you may be using to communicate over the Net, for example IRC or instant messaging.

Somebody else who's very interested in you is the marketing executive. The information they can obtain from you is done so quite legally in the vast majority of cases

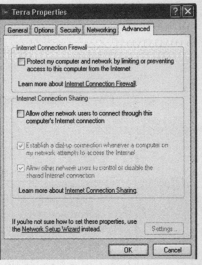

You need to make use of the Windows XP firewall if you don't already have one

but it's not always clear how and when this is being done and if you knew what was happening you probably wouldn't agree to it. You've probably heard of cookies before and this is one way that they can keep track of you and your surfing habits.

>> Understanding Cookies

Don't let the cute name fool you, cookies aren't always what they seem

We've all heard of cookies and we have a vague idea of what they do, but they're still a bit mysterious. A cookie is a small text file that's placed on your hard drive when you visit certain websites. It can then be used to track your surfing habits and activity on that site. They are used mainly by commercial sites and their purpose is twofold. After a cookie has initially been placed on your hard drive any subsequent visits to the same site will result in the cookie details being updated. The cookie will capture information such as how many times you have visited that site, and which pages you have looked at. If it's an online store it will also track any purchases you make. Apart from capturing all this marketing information, a cookie stored on your hard drive can be used to personalise web content for you. It can remember your preferences from a previous visit so that in the future, relevant items will be displayed for you and even personal greetings.

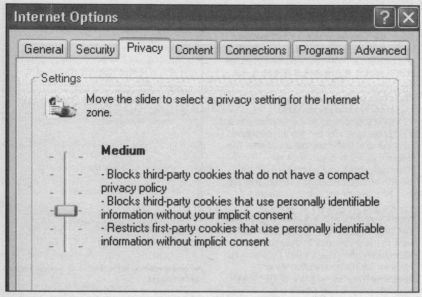

Use Privacy settings to determine how Windows XP should handle cookies

Use a firewall

We've established that your personal information is at risk both legally and illegally so you need to know how to control and even restrict the flow of this information from your PC. If you don't have one in place already you can begin by activating the Internet Connection Firewall, a welcome new feature in Windows XP. This monitors all the data that flows to and from your PC and blocks any attempts at unauthorised access to your computer.

When you first set up your connection to the internet, Windows XP asks whether you want to use the Internet Connection Firewall. If you use multiple connections then you'll need to activate the firewall for each one. To do this double click on Network Connections in Control Panel then right click on your connection and choose Properties. Select the Advanced tab and check the box under Internet Connection Firewall. It's possible to monitor the activity of your firewall although this option isn't set up by default. To create a log file, go into Network Connections, right click on your connection and choose Properties. Make sure that the Advanced tab is selected and then go down and click on Settings. Choose the Security Logging tab and under Logging Options check both boxes. While you're here, you can change the name and location of the log file if required along with the file size limit. Click on OK when you're finished.

Jargon

■ FIRST PARTY COOKIES.
This is a cookie that is being sent from the site you are viewing. First party cookies are normally used to store information about your preferences for visiting a particular site so that content can be tailored to suit you in future.

Internet Explorer Privacy Settings

Unfortunately, cookies come in all kinds of flavours and some have the ability to leave a bitter aftertaste. They can store a great deal of information about you and strip away your privacy. It's not always possible to tell who is trying to set a cookie and what their reasons for doing so are.

This is where the Privacy Settings within Internet Explorer can help by giving you control over the type of cookies, if any, that you allow to be stored on your PC. You may well be tempted to block all attempts to place cookies on your PC but this kind of action will result in you not being able to access some websites. You can access Privacy Settings by clicking on Tools, Internet Options and selecting the Privacy tab. Move the slider up and down to see which privacy setting suits you best.

Security settings

While you browse the internet and download files, the main threat to your security comes from content that's hidden within the code of an HTML page, in particular ActiveX controls. ActiveX is a programming language used on websites to enhance them with animated items such as games, images and news feeds, and an ActiveX control is an instruction that tells your PC to perform a particular task. A rogue control can have

devastating consequences on your PC so the Security tab within Internet Explorer gives you the opportunity to monitor the kind of data that's downloaded to your PC. You have four different areas that you can control: Internet, Local Intranet, Trusted Sites and Restricted Sites and for each one of you can set an individual security level.

Unless your PC forms part of a network it's unlikely that you'll need the local intranet zone. However, you will find the other three particularly useful. The default setting for the internet zone is Medium. You'll see from the information next to the slider the kind of settings that have been assigned. Click on the Custom Level button to see exactly what settings have been applied and make any adjustments that you feel are necessary.

Trusted Sites are sites that you know only contain useful and relevant information rather than harmful data. Any sites you add to this zone will be given a Low setting.

Restricted sites are those which you're not sure about. As a precaution their details can be placed in this zone so that any harmful items can be blocked should anything dangerous be downloaded when you visit the site. ∎

STEP BY STEP

≫ Adding a site to a security zone

Add one of your favourite websites as a Trusted Site, in Internet Explorer 6

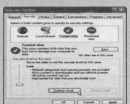

1 **CHOOSE A SAFE SITE**
Select the Trusted Sites icon and click on the Sites button. Enter the URL of the site you would like to add. If the site you're adding isn't on a secure server then uncheck Require server verification at the bottom of the dialog box and click on OK.

2 **PICK YOUR SETTINGS**
The default level for Trusted sites is low but if you have doubts about any areas of security you can click on the Custom Level button to make adjustments. As you will see nearly every setting is enabled with only a few set to Prompt.

3 **ACTIVEX CONTROLS**
One area that you should pay particular attention to is ActiveX. Instead of having Enable for any of these categories settings, set each one to Prompt instead. You can then accept ActiveX controls on a case by case basis.

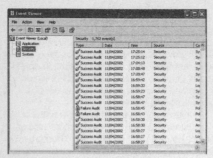

Event Viewer can track unauthorised login attempts

Ensuring internet privacy

While browsing the internet, you may have noticed a small icon appear in the Status bar at the bottom of the program Window. When this symbol is displayed, it advises you that Internet Explorer has blocked or restricted the activities of a cookie (a small piece of software that sits on your PC used by websites to identify you and monitor your online preferences) in line with the settings you have chosen within your browser.

Website privacy

To see more information on this, click on View, Privacy Report. In the dialog that appears you'll see a list of websites, all of which have content on the page you're currently viewing.

The URLs you see are of the main page you are looking at, along with those of any advertisers or marketing companies whose details it contains. Next to each one will be details of any cookies along with their status – accepted or rejected, for example. Highlight one of the sites in the list and click on Summary, and you'll be able to read their privacy policy and find out exactly what they do or don't do with information they collect. Once you've read a site's privacy policy, you

can decide whether or not you want to accept cookies for that site. You can do this by clicking on Settings in the Privacy Report dialog box and then on Edit. Enter the URL of the website in question, then click on either Block or Allow.

Bugs, not cookies

As well as cookies, your browsing habits can also be tracked using web bugs. You'll find them hidden within a graphic or an image on a web page. However, they're very difficult to spot as they are usually only one pixel in size: about as big as a full stop. The web bug is housed on a different server to the rest of a web page, usually on the system of the advertising or marketing company that placed it there.

When you click on a web page, you divulge a certain amount of information about yourself, including your IP address and the browser and operating system you are using. If the web page carries a web bug, this information will be passed on to the bug's owner, along with details of the time and date you viewed the page.

You cannot be personally identified from this information: there's no way your email address or personal contact details can be obtained. However, if a marketing company provides the web bug service to a number of different sites then it wouldn't be too difficult for them to build up a profile of you linked to your IP address.

Fortunately, you can be alerted to bugs lurking within a page you are viewing using Bugnosis, although not even this program can block them.

Security at home

Windows XP monitors the activity of your operating system using the Event Viewer. This enables you to see the information that has been recorded in the Application, Security and System logs.

There are two main reasons for using this utility: the first is to help diagnose system problems; the second is the chance to monitor activities on your PC from a security perspective. You'll find this useful when trying to detect security and privacy breaches at home. Any action carried out on the PC is recorded, along with the date, time and name of the user or process performing the action.

Event Viewer is constantly running in the background of Windows XP. To see what it's up to, go to Administrative Tools in Control Panel or type 'eventvwr.msc' in the Run dialog box. You'll see the three different logs in the left-hand pane of the window. The Security log records details of activities such as logins, file opening and creation along with the deletion of items. If an invalid login attempt is made, or if a user tries to open or create an unauthorised file, then this will all be recorded.

Viewing events

You can set preferences for each of the three event logs by highlighting them in the left pane and then clicking on View, Filter. Under the General tab, you can set a size for the file log and choose how you would like events written to the file – for example, how long they should be stored for.

A couple of columns requiring detail are Source and Event. Source records the details of the application or area of system where the event was generated. The figure

shown under Event is linked to a specific text description that you can view when looking at the properties of an event. Double click an event to see its details. The top part displays the information that you can see in the main window of Event Viewer. The text description you see here corresponds with the numerical event code. Therefore, everything displaying this number will carry the same piece of text.

Although the Security log will keep details of logins and so on, it's also worth taking a look at the Application log as well, to see which programs a user has activated. When you look at the event logs for the first time, you will see that they contain a mass of data. Click on View on the toolbar, then use Find and Filter to help you locate the information you require.

For example, using Find in the Security log, you can search for every event that has been performed by a particular user. This is ideal if you're trying to keep tabs on an individual's activity. The Filter tool enables you to perform a similar search, but with the inclusion of data criteria. You could view details of an individual's activity over a specific period. ∎

≫ Using Bugnosis to track web bugs

1 GETTING STARTED
Download a copy of the software from www.bugnosis.com.
Once it's installed, click on the Bugnosis button in the taskbar then right click in the area at the bottom of the screen and choose Options.

2 CONFIGURE BUGNOSIS
Here you will be able to set configuration options for the program. You will decide how Bugnosis should behave when a Web bug is found, and in what order results should be displayed. You can also change the image and sound files that are used to alert you.

3 HOW IT WORKS
Bugnosis will silently work away in the background until you visit a page containing a Web bug. The program will then pop up from the bottom of the screen, highlighting the offending item and giving you all the details you need so you can trace its owner if you wish.

Windows Messenger: a complete guide

85 Making the most of contacts

Organise your friends and colleagues with groups, instant alerts and personal profiles.

90 Sending sound and video online

Why simply type when you can talk and even see each other over the net?

92 Cheap online telephone calls

Talk to your friends abroad through Messenger for a fraction of the price – here's how!

Your complete guide to Windows Messenger

Windows Messenger is great for sending text messages but it can do much more than that. Get ready to really communicate...

With text messaging on mobile phones becoming more and more popular, it is no surprise that instant messaging is also proving to be such a big hit. Instead of the delays associated with email, Windows Messenger enables you to instantly see if a friend is online, and have a typed 'conversation' there and then. You can stay in touch with friends and family around the world, talk to colleagues at work and share interesting web pages you come across online – all in real time.

But instant messaging is so much more than just text: you can chat and collaborate, share your programs, files and photos, get help with your PC and see who you're talking to with a video link. And if you need to swap from email to messages or back you can do that too. It's all about communicating and you can do it all in the same place with Windows Messenger.

>> Using alerts

Find out if a friend is online or how your auction bid is doing – instantly

When you're online and signed in to Microsoft Passport, your friends and other services that use Passport can see that you're around. When you get an email in your Hotmail inbox, Hotmail can send you an alert via Windows Messenger and it shows up in the same blue alert box that pops up when one of your friends starts up their copy of Messenger or sends you a message. You'll hear a sound when contacts sign in or send you a message too.

Once you have a lot of people on your list of contacts you might not want to get those alerts; click Change in any of the alert boxes or choose Tools, Options, Preferences and you can turn off sign-in alerts, message alerts and email alerts, and turn off the sounds. To change the sound you hear, click the Sounds button, scroll through the list on the Sounds tab of the Sounds and Audio devices Properties dialog and use the Browse button to pick a new one.

You can also sign up for .NET Alerts from several websites including MSN, Expedia, lastminute.com and eBay, and more alert services are appearing all the time. Start by clicking the Alerts tab (it's got a bell icon) and clicking 'Sign Up Now' (or 'Go To Alerts Site' once you've set up alerts). You can choose whether you want to see the alerts in Windows Messenger or whether you want them as email if you're busy (or away) in Windows Messenger. If you miss an alert, it stays in the list on the Alerts tab for 24 hours. You'll see a new tab for each of the Alert services you sign up for, or you can click the folder icon at the bottom of the tab list to turn individual tabs on and off.

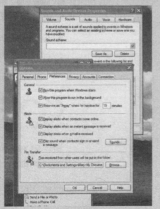

Change the bings and beeps you hear as friends log in or turn them off altogether

Windows Messenger automatically colour-codes conversations so you can see who said what. Make your own text stand out by picking your favourite font and colour and your friends will see it on their screens. Click the Font button at the bottom of any conversation, or choose Tools, Options, Personal, Change Font.

Another way to add some fun to your conversation is to use smilies – or emoticons as they're called in Windows Messenger. When you type :-) Windows Messenger turns it into a yellow smiley face for you, but you can also send little graphics of birthday presents, pets or a broken heart, etc. Just click the Emoticons button at the bottom of the conversation window and pick an icon.

There are 34 icons on the Emoticons menu and another 9 that you can check out by clicking the Help button on the menu. Try out different combinations of semi-colons, brackets and letters and you might find some extra emoticons that aren't on the menu – we found 'secret' icons for (r), (%), (?) and (#).

(Y) or (y)		:S or :S or :s or :s		(~)	
(N) or (n)		:| or :-|		(T) or (t)	
(B) or (b)		:'(		(@)	
(D) or (d)		:$ or :$		(&)	
(X) or (x)		(H) or (h)		(C) or (c)	
(Z) or (z)		:-@ or :@		(I) or (i)	
:-[or :[		(A) (a)		(S) or (s)	
(l)		(6)		(*)	
(})		(L) or (l)		(8)	
:) or :-)		(U) or (u)		(E) or (e)	
:D or :D or :d or :d :> or :>		(K) or (k)		(^)	
:O or :-O		(G) or (g)		(R) or (r)	
:P or :-p or :P or :p		(F) or (f)		(#)	
;) or ;-)		(W) or (w)		(?)	
:(or :-(		(P) or (p)		(%)	

When you first use Windows XP and sign up for a .NET Passport, Windows XP uses that information to set up Windows Messenger. Every user on your PC can have their own Passport and their own log-in for Windows Messenger. The software starts automatically when you start Windows XP and it logs on automatically when you connect to the internet, so whenever you're online your friends can see that you are. They don't have to be using Windows XP: you can contact friends who are using the MSN Messenger software.

The first thing you'll want to do is add your friends to your list of contacts. If you've already got people's contact details in your Address Book in Outlook Express, you can ask Windows Messenger to use their details from there. When you click 'Add a Contact' from the list of tasks on the main Windows Messenger screen, choose 'Search for a Contact' and fill in part of the name and Windows Messenger will find them for you.

You can also search the Hotmail Members Directory, but you have to give the first name and surname of the person you're looking for and then Windows Messenger sends them a mail saying you want to talk to them. People can also decide not to put their details in the directory. If you can remember their email, put that in instead and Windows Messenger will add them to your contacts list or tell you that they don't have a Passport account.

Who's who

Initially, Windows Messenger sorts your contacts into two groups: Online and Offline so you know whether you can send them a message or not. When one of your contacts isn't online you can still get in touch: right-

Expert Tip

■ How to talk to more than one person at once

You don't have to use MSN Chat to talk to more than one friend at once: send a message to one friend and then choose Actions, Invite Someone To This Conversation to include more people in your own online conference room.

Collaborating via the whiteboard

The whiteboard lets you show what you mean visually: you can draw and make notes on it. Either person can share a program they're working in, so you can ask your friend to help you use Microsoft Office or show them your new video editing software.

Or you can start Remote Assistance from Windows Messenger (assuming you're both using Windows XP) which lets you see what's happening on their screen, make suggestions, send them files or take over their PC to fix it.

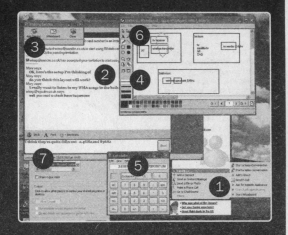

1. Start a conversation by inviting a contact to use a whiteboard or open the whiteboard whilst chatting.

2. Wait for your friend to accept your invitation.

3. Click App Sharing or Whiteboard to share a particular program or open the whiteboard.

4. You can choose any of the programs you currently have open to show or enable people use it themselves.

5. Sharing the calculator lets you both see the sums.

6. Draw, scribble and take notes on the whiteboard: you can both save it as a file on your PC at the end.

7. Meanwhile, you can carry on chatting...

click on their name and choose 'Send E-mail'. More usefully, you can divide your contacts up into groups, which is handy when you've got a long list of friends.

You can tell who's online by the colour of their icon and Windows Messenger tots up who's there and puts the number with the group name. Choose Tools, Sort Contacts By, Groups to see the default groups (Coworkers, Family, Friends and Other Contacts). You can rename or delete all of these groups except Other Contacts and add other groups to suit the way you think of the people you'll want to talk to and you can either drag names from one group to another or right-click on their name and pick 'Move Contact To' and choose the group.

Sometimes you want to have someone in

two groups, so you can minimise your list of workmates in the evening but still see if a friend from work is online to chat to: in that case hold down the Ctrl key while you drag their name or right-click and choose 'Copy Contact To'. When you add new contacts to your list they start out in Other Contacts – which is why you can't rename it.

Your list of contacts is stored by Microsoft on the internet, so you'll get your list even if you log on to Windows Messenger on another PC (at a friend's or in an internet café). But you can take a copy of your list to share with a friend or to use on a different Passport account yourself: choose File, 'Save Contact List' to export it and File, 'Import Contacts from a Saved File' to load a list you have saved.

Windows Messenger is smart enough not to duplicate names that are already in your list when you import contacts and anyone who was blocked when you saved the list will be blocked when you load it.

You can edit the exported file before you send it to a friend: they probably won't need your family or work colleagues.

One thing you can't control is the name that each of your contacts has: they get to pick that, and you can pick how people see your name in their contacts list. Choose Tools, Options, Personal, or click Personal Settings on the drop-down menu next to your name. You can have anything you like as your Display Name, even an email address – although that means anyone walking past your friend's PC could glimpse your address.

Editing profiles

Once you've installed the MSN Add-In you can use the Edit Profile button on this page to create or change your public profile on the MSN member directory. All MSN and Messenger (Windows and MSN) users can see that, not just your friends, so remember not to give out too many personal details.

You also need to decide how much information you want to give out about ways of getting in touch with you. On the Phone tab of the Preferences dialog you can fill in your home, work and mobile numbers, and they will show up along with your email when your friends right-click your name in their contacts list and choose Properties.

You can't stop people adding you to their contacts list, but you can find out when they do, stop them seeing when you're online or finding our your phone number: in Tools, Options, Privacy, make sure 'Alert me when other users add me to their contact lists' is ticked and you'll see a dialog box telling you who is adding you to their list.

You can add them to your list at the same time or you can tell Windows Messenger to block them so you always look offline to them.

You can block anyone on your contact list later, by picking their name and clicking 'Block' on the Privacy tab, and you can check back to see who has you on their contact list by clicking the View button.

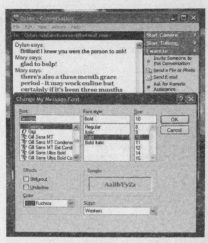

Choose your own font and colour – but remember the font has to be on your friend's PC too

And if you just don't want to talk to someone and their messages keep popping up, you can click 'Block' at the bottom of the conversation window and it will look as if you've dropped offline – don't worry, the person blocked can't tell you've blocked them so they won't be offended!

More than words

As more and more of the .NET services arrive, we'll be using Windows Messenger to manage all the ways we stay in touch with people. As well as plain text messages, you can already add video to your chat or speak to each other rather than typing.

Windows Messenger also lets you manage your Hotmail email (it's one of the features in the MSN Add-In). And while you're connecting to people online, you can send more than just text. When you're telling

Jargon

■ Passport

Microsoft's identification service – sign up with Passport and services like MSN, Hotmail and Windows Messenger know who you are, saving you time.

》MSN Messenger VS. Windows Messenger

Even if your friends don't have Windows Messenger, you can still chat

Windows XP already comes with Windows Messenger pre-installed; if you're not using Windows XP you need to download a copy of MSN Messenger from the Microsoft website.

Similarities: Both applications use .NET Passport to connect you to your friends for a chat. Windows Messenger is very similar to MSN Messenger and you can send messages back and forth between them but you don't get all of the different kinds of conversations with an MSN Messenger contact.

Differences: MSN Messenger users can make phone calls (via a provider like Net2Phone), send pages through MSN Mobile and see .NET alerts. Plus there's a handy web search toolbar at the bottom. Here's how you can communicate with friends who haven't got Windows Messenger but do have MSN Messenger.

What you can do:
■ Send text messages
■ Have a voice chat
■ Send and receive files
■ Invite several people to join a conversation

What you can't do:
■ Make a video call
■ Invite them to use Remote Assistance
■ Share applications or use the whiteboard
(you can do that with NetMeeting though)

a friend about where you went on holiday, how good your new car looks or what your new web page looks like, you could mail them the file to look at (click the Send E-mail link at the side of the conversation window).

Or you could click the link to Send a File or Photo and you'll know when the file arrives. They don't have to bother saving the file and then finding it in Explorer: Windows Messenger puts it in a directory in My Documents automatically and gives you a link to open it right away. Change where the files end up in the File Transfer filed under Tools, Options, Preferences or take a look at all the files you've received with File, Open Received Files.

Instead of just sending the file, how about collaborating on it? With the whiteboard you can both write, draw and

make notes on screen, and you both get the final result. Or you can share an application so you can show a friend how to fix red eye in their photos. Starting Remote Assistance from Windows Messenger is a good way of dealing with a friend who's nervous about letting you on their PC: you can talk them through what you're going to do before you connect to their PC and exchange passwords for the connection using Messenger.

On and off

With everything Windows Messenger can do, you'll probably want to run it whenever you start Windows XP; that way it will automatically log on when you connect to the internet. Sometimes you may not want it to start automatically, if you know you won't be online for a day or so: in that case, open Windows Messenger and choose Tools, Options, Preferences and untick 'Run this program when Windows starts' under General. But when you just want to stop people seeing that you're online, it's easier to change your status.

Click on the drop-down arrow next to your name and you can tell Windows Messenger to tell the world that you're busy, out to lunch or otherwise occupied, or you can choose to look as if you're offline. Alternatively, you can tell Windows Messenger to assume that you're away from the keyboard when you haven't used your PC for a while; the default

If none of your friends are online you can try an MSN chat room

is 15 minutes of inactivity but you can change that in Tools, Options, Preferences, 'Show me as "Away" when I'm inactive'. That way you don't come back from making a cup of tea to find frustrated messages on screen from your friends who think you're ignoring them...

MSN Add-In

To get the latest tools for Windows Messenger, you need to install Windows Messenger 4.6, then the MSN Add-Ins. Here's how to make sure you have at least version 4.6: choose Help, About Windows Messenger to check or look for a pop-up notification telling you about upgrades when you start Windows XP.

You can download the Add-In from the web (choose Tools, Add-In Web Site). When you run the installer Windows Messenger will restart and after you sign in again, you'll see an MSN entry under Tools, Add-Ins, a link to your Hotmail inbox above your contacts list and an advert at the bottom of the Windows Messenger window.

With the MSN Add-In installed, you can create or update your public profile so people can find out more about you (Tools, Options, Personal, Edit Profile) and check out your friends' profiles too (right-click on a contact and choose View Profile). You can right-click on a contact to send them an email if they're not online to talk to.

Plus you can join in chats on the MSN site: click 'Go to Chat Rooms' on the list of things you can do. Windows Messenger will download the Microsoft Chat software for you automatically; all you need to do is pick a nickname to use in the chat rooms and you can browse through the list of chats going on already or create your own personal chat room. When you find a room you like, click 'Add To My Chats' to put it in your list of favourites for next time.

There's one MSN feature you can't use yet as it's only available in the US. If you have American friends, they can register free with MSN Mobile and put in their mobile or pager number and you'll be able to send a free text message to them. Just right-click their name and choose Send a Message to a Mobile Device.

When we get MSN Mobile in the UK you'll be able to set it up by choosing Options, Phone, Mobile Settings.

Check out the .NET Alerts for ways to get at other MSN services inside Windows Messenger: you can keep an eye on your MSN Money stock portfolio, see reminders from your MSN Calendar and get the latest news from MSN Music as well as alerts from other companies.

STEP BY STEP

≫ Transferring files from one PC to another

Send a file via Windows Messenger: it's even quicker than email!

1 PICK YOUR FRIEND
Click the Send a File or Photo link in Windows Messenger. Pick one of your contacts or use Other to connect to someone new.

2 WAIT FOR THEM TO SAY YES
When you offer to send the file your friend can always decline. Only accept files from people you know and trust.

3 HERE'S THE FILE
When a file arrives, play safe and scan it for viruses before you click on the link to open it and have a look.

Voice, video & cheap phone calls in Windows Messenger

Instant messaging with Windows Messenger is great – you can see when your friends are online, send web links, exchange photos and other files and chat back and forth.

It's a lot easier to sort things out without waiting for email to arrive and replies to turn up. But sometimes you can't express yourself just by typing. Sometimes, you need to hear a friend's voice as well as just seeing the words on screen. If you're at one end of the country and you're missing your nephew's birthday party at the other end, or you want to show off your new T-shirt to a friend, a video link gets your message across so much better than a phone call.

But voice and video messages only work when the recipients are online, and you may also want to contact people who aren't online. Windows Messenger lets you do all of that, and save money on phone calls too.

If you need to chat to friends and family overseas and they have Windows XP or even an older version of Windows and MSN Messenger, you can do voice chat completely free once you're online.

Even making calls to regular phone numbers can be a lot cheaper if you use an internet call provider because your phone call can go over the internet to a country where it's cheap to make the call – and you don't have to log off first. If you've got an unlimited internet connection or a broadband line that's always on, it's ideal, but it works perfectly well on a dialup modem too.

Sending sound and video

You need a .NET Passport to use Windows Messenger: if you didn't set one up when you installed Windows XP, click the 'Get a .NET Password' link on the sign-in screen for Windows Messenger. To do internet telephony, you'll need to sign up with a provider and you can do that from within Windows Messenger. To get started with

---

⟫ Saving money with internet phone calls

You can call Australia for 3p a minute, or Bangkok for 8p! Here's how...

Video and voice chat to a PC are free, just like instant messages – you're only paying for your internet connection. However, if you're using an internet phone service like Callserve, you have to pay them for forwarding your internet call to the number you dial.

Pay by the minute: You pay by the minute, like a normal phone call, totted up in 30-second blocks – and unless you're on an unlimited connection you'll be paying for your internet phone call as well. Even so, the call charges should still be considerably lower, especially overseas.

Cheaper rates: Currently Callserve charges 3p a minute for calls to the UK, US, Hong Kong, Australia and a good few other countries, 8p a minute to Bangkok and 31p a minute to phone Egypt or a mobile phone in the UK, compared to 10p to call a mobile phone number in Iceland. It all comes down to where Callserve has its local connection and how much it costs for the phone calls in that country.

No line rental: There aren't any other charges for running the account or line rental, so you know exactly how much calls will cost. Other internet telephone charges are roughly similar. With Callserve you have to buy time in advance, like a mobile phone voucher: you can buy £10 or £20 at a time on the website and when you start running out of units it will warn you to go and top up.

Password protected: You'll need to remember a PIN number, which should stop anyone else using up your phone calls, and you can see the last ten calls you've made or get a full monthly statement on the Callserve website so you know exactly where the money is going.

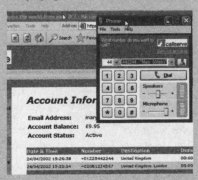

With a Callserve account you need to charge up your balance in advance, then dial away

---

video and voice chat, all you need is the hardware and someone to call.

Like most things in Windows XP, Windows Messenger lets you work in several different ways; you can right-click on a name in your contact list and choose 'Start a Voice Conversation' or 'Start a Video Conversation' or click 'More' in the 'I want to...' pane to pick Voice or Video Conversation and then pick a friend to chat to. And if you're already chatting away in text, if you've got a webcam, you can add voice or video to the chat by clicking 'Start Talking' for voice or 'Start Camera' for video and voice.

If you have a webcam, you can send video to friends as you chat. It works best if you have broadband but it's still acceptable over 56K.

Accepting the call

However you start the chat, the person at the other end has to accept your invitation to chat before Windows Messenger starts sending sound and video. They can click on the word Accept in the on-screen invitation, hit Alt+T or click their own Start Camera button to accept.

If they can't accept your video chat invitation because they're not running Windows XP, Windows Messenger will tell you that's why. If they're behind a firewall that won't let the connection through, Windows Messenger will try to make the connection and then tell you the conversation has ended. Look for the words 'Connection established' on the status line of your chat window.

If you don't run the audio and video tuning wizard (from Tools, Audio Tuning Wizard) before you start your first call, Windows XP runs it for you automatically: you can check your camera is working and set up the microphone and speakers so the volume is comfortable and doesn't cause feedback. Unless you're using headphones, Windows XP does audio echo cancellation to stop you picking up echoes from your speakers on the microphone, which can be very disconcerting.

Working together

Both of you work in the same way, with controls at the side of the screen for the sound and camera, but if you start a conversation as video you can't change it to a voice conversation by clicking Stop

Camera: that turns off sound and video together. Instead, you need to click the Options drop-down on the video window and choose Stop Sending Video, and they'll see either a frozen image or a black screen at the other end but you can both still talk.

You can carry on typing while you talk – if you want to share a web link or send an emoticon, for example – and the chat connection stays live even if you turn off the camera and microphone.

If you want to keep an eye on the image you're sending out, click Options and choose 'Show My Video as Picture-in-Picture' to get a thumbnail in the corner of the image.

Keep an eye on the speaker and microphone levels at the side of the screen; if they're very high or low you can change the volume from here or run the tuning wizard again from the View menu. If you can't see the controls at all, choose View, Sidebar to display them.

Jargon

■ Ports

Your connection to the Internet is really lots of individual, numbered connections using TCP/IP (Transmission Control Protocol/Internet Protocol) and UDP (User Datagram Protocol) to talk to other computers; each connection is called a port and you can block or open individual ports in your firewall.

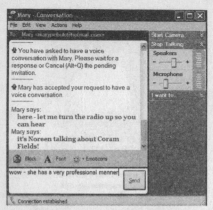

Use a voice chat when you want to share a sound, hear someone's voice or when they're not using Windows XP so you can't do video chat

Making cheaper phone calls

Voice chat is great when your friends are online, but if you want to phone a real phone number and have a good old-fashioned conversation, choose Actions, Make a Phone Call to open the Phone tool. The first time you try, Windows Messenger checks that your internet connection lets you make calls (some firewalls may block you) and then asks you to choose a Voice Service Provider.

If you haven't signed up yet, click on the Callserve logo (the main UK phone partner for Windows XP) and you'll find yourself on Callserve's site, already logged in via Passport and ready to sign up for the service and buy some phone time. When you buy £10 worth of phone time, Callserve

Jargon

■ POTS

You've heard of ADSL, ISDN and other fast new digital telephone lines, but what's the official term for the standard analog 'plug the phone into the socket' telephone line? It's called POTS – Plain Old Telephone Service! And the voice quality on a phone is just 8kHz and mono to boot: compared to FM radio at 11kHz stereo and CD at 15kHz stereo.

sends you a free headset, or you can buy the £30 xpPhone handset, which makes it feel much more like using a real phone.

Once you've set up your account you get a PIN number to type in, to stop anyone else using your phone credits. To make a call, you can type in the number or click the little buddy icon to pick from the contacts on your list who've published their phone numbers. The Phone dialog remembers numbers you've called recently too, even if you weren't able to get through, so you can pick from the drop-down list.

Because it's an international service, you need to pick the country code for the number you're dialling, even if it's in the UK. If you don't, the country code list pops up automatically for you to pick from and it remembers the last code you picked.

When you click Dial, it's just like making a normal phone call without hearing the dial tone: just like a phone box, you can see how long the call has lasted and how much money you've got left. If the number's engaged you'll see an error message – and you'll hear it too, although rather than a busy tone you get a spoken message from Callserve. You can change the volume with the same controls as in voice and video chat. Press Hang Up when you're done.

If you want to see how many calls you've been making and how much they've cost you, click View my account. When you're running low on money, you'll get a prompt to buy more time: you can top up your phone credit quickly, because the Callserve site stores your credit card details for you.

What makes tools like Windows Messenger so useful is something called the 'network effect'; the more of your friends and family you can contact through it, the more you'll use it. With the internet phone tool, you can reach anyone, even if they're not using Windows or MSN Messenger. You may never pick up the telephone again!

Added extras and fun customisation

Want to keep a record of your IM conversations? Would you like to have a custom away message instead of the standard ones? Need to minimise your conversations quickly when someone walks up to your PC while you're having a particularly private chat? Try the Plus! Extension for Windows Messenger. It's not from Microsoft, but it's a handy extra tool that you can download from www.patchou.com/msgplus/download.htm.

If you want an image that's not the way you really look, take a peak at the 3D avatars in SeeStorm Messenger (ssm. seestorm.com/download/): you can look like an alien, Santa Claus or a pumpkin or pay for extra avatars. When you install SeeStorm it puts another option in your 'I want to...' list – 'Start 3D-character conferencing' – which fires up the SeeStorm window complete with talking head.

Tweaker (www.kgareth.com) is fun – you can change your nickname repeatedly, have it scroll or flash on your friends' screens and send lots of emoticons – but it's useful too, if you want to choose your away message or set up automatic responses to save you typing 'hi there!' every time someone says 'hello' to you.

If you want to change your nickname automatically, based on the time, the date or the music you're listening to, try MySweetNix! (www.aalaap.com), which does text effects too.

Also useful are the shortcuts you can define with Advanced Messenger Plus, so you don't have to type things out in full every time; it also keeps a log of your conversations – and it can read them out so you don't miss anything if you lose them behind other windows. Fonix Extensions is another useful program that also enables you to set Away messages and it keeps track of everyone contacting you; you can also ensure you log in with the same status so you can stay invisible even if you lose your internet connection and have to redial.

You can have more than one .NET Passport and more than one Windows Messenger login, but you can only use one at once – unless you use MSN Polygamy (www.asdfuae.tk) which lets you open as many copies of Windows Messenger as you like. This is very handy if you have a work and a home name and you want to log on with both at once! ∎

≫ Keeping a conversation private

All your video chats can be just as secure as a normal phone call

Using a webcam for video chat isn't like having a webcam on your website where you're always sending up images. The webcam only works when you click the Start Camera button on the chat screen and you can turn the camera or the sound off at any point you want.

Staying secure: Windows Messenger doesn't give out extra information about you or your connection and you'll be protected by the Windows XP Internet Connection Firewall – but you should still be careful you don't give away your password or too much personal information when you're chatting to acquaintances online. If you're using a different firewall you'll need to make changes to the settings to let Windows Messenger send voice and video info through it.

Top tip: Only accept files from people you know and find out what the file is and then virus-check it. If you put your phone number on your profile to let people get in touch with you by phone, only people on your contact list will see the number.

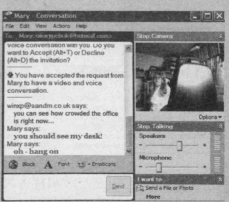

When you invite a friend to have a video chat they get the chance to say yes or no. Either of you can turn the camera off at any point, if you're not feeling presentable enough!

Making phone calls with Windows Messenger

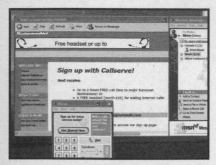

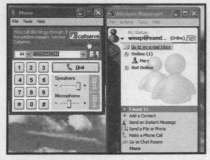

1 SIGN UP WITH CALLSERVE
Choose 'Make a Phone Call' from the 'I want to...' list in Windows Messenger and Windows XP checks that you're connected then asks you to pick a partner to make your phone calls through: you'll need to register and use your credit card to buy phone time.

2 DIAL BY HAND
Pick the country code from the drop-down list and type in the number without the 0 at the beginning for UK numbers, then click Dial. If the number is busy or unavailable you'll hear a short message and see an error on screen too. The number is stored so it's quick to redial.

4 HAVE A CHAT
Once your call is through you'll see how long you've been talking and what your balance is. If you run out of money you can click the links to the Callserve site to top up your account. You can adjust the volume from here if you need to – or just relax and have a chat.

5 DIAL AGAIN
The last number you called stays in the Phone dialog and other numbers you've called before are in a drop-down list – just click the arrow to scroll through them. You can see the name and which number is which for phone numbers that come from your contacts list.

HAVING PROBLEMS WITH WINDOWS MESSENGER?

http://support.microsoft.com/default.aspx?xmlid=fh%3BEN-US%3Bwinmsgr

3 PHONE A BUDDY
Click the little buddy icon above the Dial button to get a list of people on your contact list who've published their phone numbers for you to call: you can give your own home, work and mobile numbers to your friends by choosing Tools, Publish My Phone Numbers.

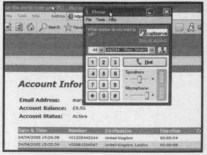

6 CHECK YOUR STATEMENT
Click on 'View my account' to see details of your account including your current balance and your last 10 calls – you can see who, where, when and how much. For details of previous calls click Monthly Statement or go to User Settings to change your contact or credit card details.

Jargon

■ VOIP

Voice over IP is another term for internet telephony; instead of dialling another phone directly, you connect to the internet and send a digital signal to a phone service that turns it into a phone call from wherever it's cheapest.

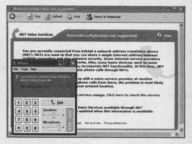

If you're using ADSL from work, you may have trouble using Windows Messenger for phone calls: ask about up-to-date NAT devices to fix it

The ABC of Upgrading

ABC of upgrading

If you can change a fuse, you can upgrade a PC.
It's as simple as that. So, roll up your sleeves
and follow our basic step-by-step guide

Computers are made for opening up. This is good news because almost every other item of consumer electronics – from your video recorder to your TV – isn't. PCs are specifically designed to be different and the reason for this is to enable you to easily upgrade.

By upgrading, you can turn an old PC into a new one at a huge cost saving. Even if your ambitions are more basic than that – limited to a new 3D card to play the latest games for instance – your PC has been designed to make that easy. Provided you take basic common sense steps, you don't have to worry about electric shocks or causing irreparable damage that is an issue with other types of electrical goods.

So, the basics. The first thing to get in mind is how a PC is put together. The hardware is the stuff inside the PC itself, like 3D cards, memory, the hard disk and so on. This is upgraded by opening the case in the manner described overleaf, and installing new versions.

When you install a new piece of hardware and turn the PC back on, the operating system Windows XP recognises it and sets it up to work properly. Indeed, one of the main reasons for getting Windows XP is that it makes the process of installing and using new hardware very easy indeed.

The final element of the equation is your applications software, which you use to actually gain the benefit of your new hardware. However, for the purposes of this feature, we'll assume you know how to install a program and concentrate mainly on the process of upgrading to new hardware, and the tools within Windows XP to make it work effortlessly.

Why upgrade?

■ Boost performance
Time stands still for nobody and this is even more true for PCs. New software often requires new hardware.

■ Do new things
Do you want to get into video editing or home networking, for example? You may need to install new hardware.

■ Repair broken bits
If something goes wrong, just replace it!

■ Avoid buying a new PC
There's a point at which even the most souped-up PC can't be upgraded any longer and has to be replaced, but for the most part, it's hugely cheaper to replace individual bits as you go rather than throw the whole thing out.

Getting prepared

You shouldn't skip this stage. Lack of preparation is the single biggest cause of problems later. The very first thing you should do is backup your files. The best way to do this is use a CD burner to copy files from your hard drive onto a blank CD, using the CD burning features within Windows XP. If you don't have a CD burner, a ZIP drive or equivalent will do (it'll just be slightly less convenient).

Next, we'd normally recommend

≫ Opening a PC and handling hardware

Don't be nervous, PCs are made for opening. Here's how to do it

First things first: switch off your PC and unplug it. Unplug all the other cables. Then place it on a clean, dust-free, level surface. Most PCs today have removable panels which enable you to gain easy access to the innards. If you have a tower system (that is, the PC stands vertically), the chances are there's either a quick release catch or simple screw to undo to take the side off.

It's unlikely you will need to wield a screwdriver for a system built for home use, but if you do, it's not a problem – just try not to lose any screws!

If it's a desktop unit, i.e. it sits horizontally on your desk with your monitor on top, then

it's a case of undoing some screws located at the back. Handling the hardware itself is pretty easy. The rule here is to hold any hardware by the edges. Try not to touch any of the surfaces – although it's unlikely you'll do any damage, there is an outside chance of static on your hands damaging the electronics. One further thing you can do to eliminate this risk, is to wear an anti-static bracelet – buy one from PCWorld, they're only a few quid. Then just install the hardware using the guides overleaf.

Post-upgrade

After you've successfully inserted the cards, connected in any new drives or whatever, reassemble the PC, plug everything back in and turn it on.

If all's gone well, Windows XP will start. Once it's booted up, you need to ensure the correct drivers are installed. This used to be a difficult and time-consuming job, but no longer. One of the key benefits of Windows XP is it makes installing and managing drivers very simple. For the most part, Windows XP should simply detect any new hardware, connect itself to the internet and download the appropriate drivers from the Microsoft website (where there's a constantly updated list of approved drivers).

If this doesn't happen, or there's a problem with a driver which causes system errors, you can use the built-in Driver Rollback and troubleshooter features to solve them. It's pretty unlikely this will happen to you – but just in case, there's a full guide to the upgrading features in Windows XP within this feature.

making a Windows Startup disk. This is a floppy disk which, in the event of a serious problem that prevents Windows XP from loading properly, can get your system up and running for you to make repairs. However, you don't need one in Windows XP because the Windows CD does it for you. Broadly speaking, there are four types of upgrade we're interested in: slot upgrades (equipment like 3D cards, network cards, sound cards which fit into expansion slots); memory upgrades; hard disk upgrades; and CD/DVD/CD-R drive upgrades. Each of these requires a different approach.

Over the next few pages, we'll show you what the differences are and how to safely upgrade your computer, from opening up your PC, to installing the correct drivers so that your new hardware works perfectly.

Upgrading a graphics card

When it comes to upgrading your graphics card you need to be aware of two things. First, is your existing graphics card built into your motherboard, or is it a card that can be easily removed?

To find out what kind of graphics card you have, power down your PC. Remove the case and find out where your monitor lead plugs in. If it plugs into a socket that's attached to a card then that's your existing graphics card. If not, then your motherboard has the graphics card built-in. If this is the case then you will need to disable this before you physically install your new card.

The second question is which slots are available to put a new graphics card into? There are two types of slot – one brown and several white ones. The brown slot is a dedicated port for graphics cards and is

>> Upgrade now or later?

Technology marches on, so is it worth getting an upgrade or waiting?

Graphics cards

■ **What effect?**
Whether we admit it or not, one of the main uses for our PCs at home is a very expensive and cutting edge games machine. If you're finding 3D applications are starting to slow down, or that you're needing to set options to their lowest defaults to get the latest games working, a new graphics card will make an enormous amount of difference. If you're still using a graphics card that's a couple of years old, there's a whole world of special effects you're missing out on.

■ **Recommended**
As far as performance graphics cards go, nVidia has had the market sewn up for some time now. It has just released its GeForce 4 range. In terms of price and performance, the GeForce4 MX is the best budget card, the GeForce3 Ti the best mid range, and the GeForce4 Ti the highest performing. We recommend the Sparkle GeForce4 Ti 4400 – at around £280 it's a bargain. Or see what arch-rival ATI brings out next...

Internet connection

■ **What effect?** The impact of broadband is still to be felt in this country, but when you get it, expect it to change the way you use your PC. Fast download speeds – a steady 500Kbps is normal, around ten times the speed of a 56K modem – make the transfer of large files to and from work a cinch, and open up a whole world of convenient online music and video. And if you're an online gamer, you'll suddenly start to play well. Trust us.

■ **Recommended**
There are only really two choices for broadband at the moment – via a fibre-optic cable or through your telephone line with ADSL. Alternatives include satellite receivers, although these are still prohibitively expensive for home use. If you live in a cabled area, this option is usually cheaper, faster and more reliable than upgrading your phone line to ADSL, although BT's latest wholesale price reduction should see this change soon.

DVD writers

■ **What effect?**
If you've been thinking about adding a CD writer to your PC setup, have a think about DVD instead. A new generation of disc drives allows you to burn information onto DVDs, whether it's creating a DVD-ROM full of data or, better still, a DVD Video with movies. With the right software, such as VideoWave 5, you can convert digital video filmed on a DV camcorder

into DVD format, then design and add an interface to select movies or chapters. The DVD will play on virtually any consumer DVD player, so you can watch your own home movies on TV. DVDs also make a fantastic way to archive digital photos.

■ **Recommended**
Pioneer's DVD-A03 was the first affordable DVD writer, and costs around £388 (£330 excluding VAT). It's able to burn data or movies onto both DVD-Rs, which can be written just once, or DVD-RWs, one of a few rival formats for rewritable DVDs. It also reads and writes CD-Rs and CD-RWs.

System memory

■ **What effect?** The fastest, cheapest and most effective upgrade you can make to your PC is adding more RAM. Purchased in sticks known as DIMMs, your PC will use either single or double data rate modules, in a variety of speeds. If you have a Pentium 4 system, it's likely that you'll need the pricier but even quicker Rambus type chips. Check your documentation to find out what sort you need, then simply drop in more sticks of the correct variety.

■ **Recommended**
When looking for RAM, there's not a huge difference in performance between brands. Unless you're looking at running a server, our advice is to go for the best value. Crucial.com is a good site for SDRAM, but doesn't stock Rambus memory. Other brands of repute include Kingston, Micron and Samsung. Buying over the counter has been more expensive, although major chains have reduced their prices over the years.

Sound

■ **What effect?**
It's amazing how little we appreciate the sounds that emit from our computer. Although if you're still using the speakers which came with your PC, it's slightly more understandable. Generally speaking, this is one area where PC manufacturers cut costs, and while your soundcard probably supports the likes of Dolby Digital surround sound and a massive tonal range, it's likely your speakers don't.

■ **Recommended**
While you generally get what you pay for with most hi-fi equipment, when it comes to PC speakers you can find some excellent quality kit at the sub £100 mark. If you watch a lot of movies on your PC, you may want to consider the more expensive 5.1 'home theatre' style sets with digital inputs and so on, but otherwise we recommend the Cyber Acoustics CA-440E. At just £40 for a set of Dolby 5.1 speakers, it's a steal.

White slots are for PCI cards – push the card in firmly

assistant find the card you need!

Now all you need to do is choose the card itself. Although there are many different makes, most cards are based on one of two designs (known as chipsets): GeForce and ATI. At the moment, the latest chipsets are the GeForce 4 and ATI 8500, but if you're working to a tight budget, consider a basic GeForce 2-based card – these can cost less than £50.

Adding memory to your PC

Like everything else in computing, memory has evolved over the past few years. There are currently three different standards available for desktop PCs, and one more for laptops. Your PC will only support one type of memory, so it's important you choose the correct one for your computer. Thankfully it's quite easy to track down what memory is used by your PC. All you need to know is your PC or motherboard's model, which you should find in your PC's manual.

Armed with this information, log on to www.crucial.com/uk/ and select either Personal Computing or Motherboards &

called AGP; the white slots are PCI, and are used for all manner of cards, including soundcards and modems. For the record, AGP cards offer better performance, so if you have an AGP slot use it, but if you have onboard graphics then you may find that only PCI slots are available, in which case get a PCI card. If you're not sure where to look, just make sure you know which card you're after, and let the shop

>> Upgrading a graphics card

Improve your computer's visual capabilities in one easy upgrade

1 To disable any onboard graphics, consult your manual. Press the key that's prompted to enter setup when you boot. Look for a Video Configuration option (in the Advanced Chipset or Integrated Peripherals menus) and disable it. Save changes, exit and switch off.

2 Fitting your new graphics card is the same as any other expansion card. Just locate the AGP or PCI slot, remove any backing plate, then gently, but firmly, push the card into place. Check it's seated snugly then secure it to the case as shown.

3 Now reboot your PC and Windows should automatically detect your new card. Now for the drivers. If Windows refuses to let you install the drivers, click Driver Signing under the Hardware tab of System Properties and set it to Warn instead of Block

only upgrade RD-RAM chips in pairs. So, if you want to add 128MB of RAM, you have to buy two 64MB RD-RAM chips.

Each type of memory is also available in different speeds – it's best to choose the fastest your PC will support. The Crucial Memory Selector only displays memory that's compatible with your PC, so you know it's suitable.

Finally, laptops use a different type of chip again – SO-DIMMs. There is another advantage to expanding your laptop's memory – more memory reduces hard-drive access, which means less battery power is wasted in normal everyday use.

RAID Cards before clicking Go. You can then choose your model and identify what you need, and even order it from here.

There are currently three different types of memory for desktop PCs: SD-RAM, DDR-RAM and RD-RAM (or Rambus). The acronyms are unimportant, as the Crucial Memory Selector tells you which one you need. What you do need to know is that while SD-RAM and DDR-RAM chips can be upgraded one at a time, you can

Adding a new CD/DVD drive

If you've still got a standard CD drive, you may wonder why you need to upgrade. If you want to play DVD movies on your PC you should get a DVD player. If you want to write your own CDs – you want a back-up device, or want to send large files to friends and family, for instance – then consider investing in a CD Re-writer. You can buy internal and external models – the

>> Adding memory to your PC
One of the most common upgrades – here's how to do it simply

1 When you come to install your new memory you'll notice some slots at the bottom of the chip. These should line up with the slots on the memory socket – don't try forcing the memory in without lining it up first as you risk damaging both memory and motherboard.

2 Once you've got the memory the correct way round, make sure the socket clips are fully pushed back, then line up the memory chip and push down firmly into place. The clips should click into position if the memory is seated correctly. The process is identical for SD-RAM, DDR-RAM and RD-RAM.

3 Laptop memory has to be installed at a 45-degree angle, then pushed down until it locks into the side clips. Finding where it goes can be tricky: your laptop's manual should help, and most memory sockets are easily accessible from a flap on the base. See www.crucial.com/uk/install/sodimm.asp for more info.

≫ Adding a new CD/DVD drive

Get the best music and movies directly through your PC

1 There's a cable for connecting your CD drive to your soundcard so you can listen to audio CDs through your PC's speakers. Connect one end to the free slot on the back of your CD drive as shown here.

2 The other end of the cable goes into an appropriate slot on your soundcard (or the motherboard, if it has onboard sound). If there is more than one slot available, consult your soundcard or motherboard manual to find out which slot it should go in.

3 If you want to play DVD movies on your PC you'll need some extra software like SoftDVD Max from MGI. When you first use your DVD player you may be able to watch multi-region DVDs, but this is a time-limited feature, so make sure it's set to Region 2 for the UK.

latter are easy to set up, but don't offer much in the way of performance and are relatively expensive. Look for a model that has speeds of 40x read, 24x write and 16x re-write, and make sure it has burn-proof technology.

Fitting your new drive is identical to fitting a hard drive – both share the same cables and connectors. We recommend keeping your hard drive on a separate channel to your CD drives – your new drive should come with a cable if only one is currently in use. If your current CD drive shares the same channel as your hard drive, now is the perfect time to move it to the new channel. Set your new drive's jumpers to master and attach it to its own channel, then just plug in the old drive – which should be set to slave already – to the same cable as your new CD drive.

If you're replacing your existing drive, you should be left with just two devices – one hard drive and your new drive – attached to different channels. Both should be set to master. See the boxout for information on connecting them up and making sure your new drive is detected by

your PC. In this case you're looking for the Secondary Master settings (and Secondary Slave if you've moved your existing CD drive on to this channel).

Adding a new hard drive

There is one thing you should consider before purchasing your hard drive. Is there space in your PC to house it? All drives are housed in special bays, which come in two sizes: 3.5-inch and 5.25-inch. Floppy

Upgrading a CD drive is slightly more technical than it first appears

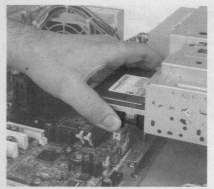

and hard drives are 3.5-inch. It's a good idea to open your case to check you have a spare 3.5-inch bay before purchase – if not, ask your supplier to add a special mounting kit to your order so you can house it in a 5.25-inch bay.

Up to four drives – hard or CD/DVD – can be connected internally to your PC.

These four drives are connected by way of two ribbons that plug into two interfaces (or channels as they're known) on your PC's motherboard. Each channel has up to two devices attached to it. Because two devices are sharing the same channel, your PC needs to know which one has priority over the other. This is achieved by making one device the 'master', and the second device the 'slave'. By default your existing hard drive is set up as a master device, so that the PC recognises it first and knows to load Windows from that hard drive. Therefore you should set up your new drive as the slave.

Now mount the hard drive in an available bay and find the cable that connects your existing hard drive to the motherboard – there'll be an extra connector on this which plugs into the back of your new drive. You also need a spare power connector for the drive.

To set up your new drive once Windows

STEP BY STEP

>> Master/slave settings

The simple way to get your new hard drive installed and running

1 You set your new hard drive to 'slave' by setting some jumpers at the back of the drive – a pair of tweezers is handy here. To find out what setting to use, check the back of your drive or the hard drive manual. If you can't find anything, note the hard drive's manufacturer and the model number, then go to www.itechs-systems.com/pages/ dmj.htm where you'll find all the links you need.

2 Plugging in the power cables is simple – just find a spare cable that's the same as that used by your other hard drive. It's shaped so it can only fit one way. Modern interface cables are designed the same way with a notch at the top, but if your cable doesn't have this or you don't know which way to plug in the cable, make sure the red stripe running down the cable is positioned closest to the power supply.

3 When you reboot your PC, your new drive should be automatically detected before Windows loads. If not, press the key shown to enter the set-up program (often [Del], [F1] or [F2]). Look for your hard drive settings – usually under Main Settings, and make sure the Primary Slave setting is set to Auto. Save your changes, exit and restart your PC. It should now be detected and you can set it up in Windows.

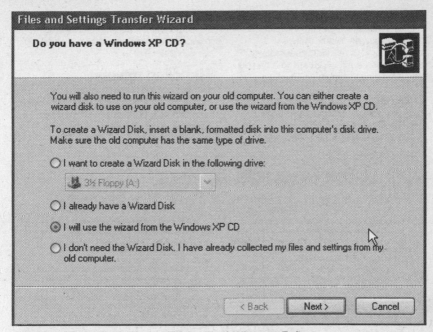

Files and Settings Transfer Wizard

Do you have a Windows XP CD?

You will also need to run this wizard on your old computer. You can either create a wizard disk to use on your old computer, or use the wizard from the Windows XP CD.

To create a Wizard Disk, insert a blank, formatted disk into this computer's disk drive. Make sure the old computer has the same type of drive.

◯ I want to create a Wizard Disk in the following drive:

[3½ Floppy (A:)]

◯ I already have a Wizard Disk

⦿ I will use the wizard from the Windows XP CD

◯ I don't need the Wizard Disk. I have already collected my files and settings from my old computer.

[< Back] [Next >] [Cancel]

Use the Files and Settings Transfer Wizard to set Windows XP up just the way you like it

loads, click on Start, Help and Support, and type in 'disk management'. Under Suggested Topics, click on Disk Management under Overviews, Articles and Tutorials, then click 'Checklist: Adding a new disk' and follow its instructions.

Upgrade tools within Windows XP

There comes a time in every computer owner's life when they want to get more from their PC by adding more devices or programs. New devices, such as printers, scanners or modems, require drivers: software programs that tell the operating system how to work the new equipment.

In times past, you needed to make sure that your computer could recognise the new hardware, then find an appropriate device driver and install it without creating conflicts with the computer's other equipment. Any upgrade of operating system, like a move from an earlier version of Windows to Windows XP

usually means replacing some or all of your drivers.

Thankfully, Windows XP makes life easy. It is the best Windows yet for adding new devices. In most cases when you want to add a new device, Windows XP will identify it and install the appropriate software automatically. The Windows XP CD is jam packed with device drivers for a wide range of equipment, so the term 'plug and play' really describes how it works. Unfortunately, there are still times when you might run into problems. You may need to add an older device to your PC that Windows XP cannot recognise, or

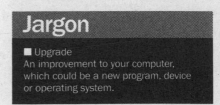

Jargon

■ Upgrade
An improvement to your computer, which could be a new program, device or operating system.

you may have bought equipment that isn't recommended for use with Windows XP. If you find yourself in one of these situations, all is not lost, as Windows XP contains some nifty features to help you get around such problems.

Upgrading to Windows XP

Upgrade Advisor is aimed at people wanting to upgrade to Windows XP from an older Windows. It smoothes the transition by preparing you for any incompatibilities before you upgrade. Take a look at the Upgrade Advisor box below for more details.

Handling drivers

Driver handling is much improved in Windows XP. It helps you to find drivers for your devices, notifies you when driver updates occur and lets you roll back to an earlier driver version if a new driver

≫ Using Upgrade Advisor

A one-stop check to ensure Windows XP can handle your hardware

If you've yet to upgrade to Windows XP, Upgrade Advisor is a great program that runs under your older version of Windows. It checks your system thoroughly and reports potential hardware and software problems that you might encounter during the upgrade.

This is a great idea, because you can then find out how to sort out any incompatibilities with your system before you upgrade.

RUN UPGRADE ADVISOR
Choose 'Check system compatibility' to run Upgrade Advisor

You can find Upgrade Advisor on any Windows XP CD (we've also featured it on previous cover CDs of this magazine), or you can download the most recent version from: www.microsoft.com/windowsxp/pro/howtobuy/upgrading/advisor.asp

To start Upgrade Advisor from a Windows XP CD, put the CD into your computer's CD ROM drive, and it should auto run. From the Windows XP welcome screen, choose 'Check system compatibility'. Upgrade Advisor then asks to connect to the internet. Choose 'Yes', to download the updated set up files. It's important to follow this step, as compatibility problems that existed when your CD was made may well have been sorted out by now. The program then connects to Microsoft, gets the updates and installs them. No information about your computer is sent to Microsoft; there is no need to worry about privacy issues.

Once updated, Upgrade Advisor checks the hardware and software in your computer and creates a detailed report. This tells you what hardware you have that might need new drivers. It says which software will need to be reinstalled after the upgrade and which software may need replacing. You can print out the report and use it to ensure you have the right software CDs to make your upgrade as painless as possible.

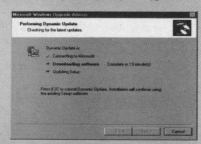

GET THE LATEST UPDATES
Upgrade Advisor gets the latest updates directly from Microsoft's website

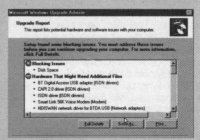

UPGRADE REPORT
Upgrade Advisor gives you a detailed report on your system's compatibility

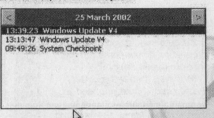

Dates marked in bold show days with restore points that you can use System Restore to return your computer to

doesn't work. Try to use devices that have been tested on Windows XP, or at least drivers that were written for Windows XP. To find out more about device drivers and how to handle them, see the Drivers box.

Transferring settings

When you start out using Windows XP, you don't want to waste time setting up internet connections, other configurations and transferring files from your old computer. The Files and Settings Transfer Wizard does all that for you.

Select Start, All Programs, Accessories, System Tools, and Files and Settings Transfer Wizard. It takes you through step by step the process of transferring everything you need. It doesn't matter if the other computer is running an older version of Windows, as the wizard creates a floppy disk that will run on the other computer.

Recover from disaster

System Restore is a fantastic feature of Windows XP. It allows you to roll all your system settings back in time to when everything was last working properly, but it

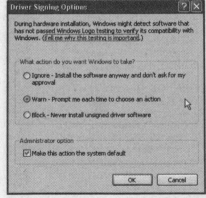

Use driver signing to ensure your device drivers are compatible with Windows XP

doesn't roll back your files. If disaster strikes when performing an upgrade for example, and your computer stops working as well as it should, use System Restore to take you back. Select Start, Help and Support, 'Undo Changes to your computer with System Restore'. Now choose 'Restore my computer to an earlier time' and click Next. You then see a calendar with some dates in bold. The bold days are days that have restore points, times when Windows XP detected that the system was stable. Choose a restore point before the trouble started and click Next to roll your computer back to then.

Consider setting a restore point if you ever feel that your computer is running smoothly and you're happy with it.

System information

There's no reason other than curiosity to look at your system information if your computer has not developed a fault.

However, it's always better to be prepared should you need to do some detective work. Go to Start, Control Panel, 'Printers and other hardware', and choose System from the bottom of the left-hand pane.

This calls up the system properties dialog, from which you can view hardware settings (see our guide to Device Manager in the Drivers box), system restore information or Windows Update settings to name but three. It's best to ensure that automatic updates are enabled from the Automatic Updates tab.

This will check for system updates from Microsoft whenever your computer connects to the internet. Look at each of the tabs and become acquainted with what they do.

It's unlikely that you'll need to mess around with the settings as Windows XP usually takes care of such under-the-bonnet matters itself, but it is useful to know what they do in case you need to get your hands dirty.

Adding hardware

Windows XP usually controls the process of adding new devices to

Program compatibilty

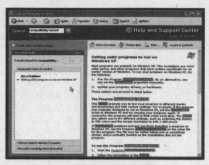

1 LAUNCH THE WIZARD
Go to Start, Help and Support and type Compatibility Wizard into the search bar. Press Enter and launch the wizard from the link in the help text.

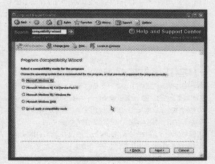

4 CHOOSE THE EMULATOR
Choose the version of Windows the program last worked with. The compatibility Wizard will help Windows XP to emulate the settings of an earlier Windows. Now click Next.

FILES & SETTINGS (1)

You can move all your work and set-up from one computer to another by using the Files and Settings Transfer Wizard, in the Accessories folder.

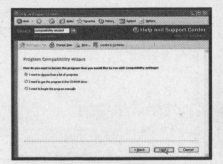

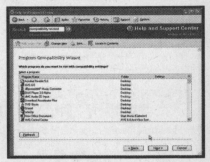

2 **LIST YOUR PROGRAMS**
When the wizard starts, click Next. If the
program is already installed on your
computer, choose from a list of programs; if not,
choose to locate the program manually.

3 **LOCATE YOUR PROGRAM**
Choose the incompatible program from the
list. If you can't find it here, click Back and
locate the program manually. The manual
selection requires you to browse for the
executable program file. Click Next.

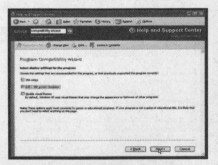

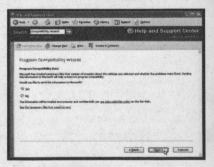

5 **CHOOSE DISPLAY OPTIONS**
If you aren't sure of the colour and
resolution your program used, go for trial
and error. Select some probable settings and click
Next. Test the program – if it doesn't work, go
back and change the settings.

6 **CONFIRM AND SAVE**
Once happy, choose to always use these
settings for this program and click Next.
Microsoft can improve Windows XP, if you send
them details of the program's compatibility
settings. Send them and finish.

FILES & SETTINGS (2)

This wizard will save all the settings and files for burning
to a CD or will transfer all the information across a
network or a serial connection, so you can carry on as if
nothing has changed but on a different computer.

your computer. With USB ports standard amongst today's computers, you may not even have to open your computer up to install something – just feed it a driver CD and away you go.

However, if your devices are older than the modern standard, or your drivers aren't up to scratch, you might need to do a little more than put your feet up and play with your new gadget.

If your hardware isn't automatically detected, go to Control Panel, choose

'Printers and other hardware' and then select Add Hardware from the See Also pane on the left. This starts the Add Hardware wizard.

Adding hardware

This will scan your computer for new hardware and help you to install it. If the wizard doesn't detect your hardware, look for it in Device Manager (see the Drivers box for details).

If there is no entry for the hardware in

➤➤ Solving problems with drivers

Finding drivers can be tricky, but Windows XP will help you out

Most device drivers for your computer will be installed when you upgrade to Windows XP. If your computer came with Windows XP pre-installed, all your devices should be correctly set up, and you should have no major worries. Areas where driver difficulties do crop up are typically with internal modems or legacy devices like video capture cards that were developed for older versions of Windows.

If you intend to buy a new device, the best way to ensure it will work, is to check to see it is listed on the Microsoft hardware compatibility list. You can find this at www.microsoft.com/hcl/default.asp. The list is fully searchable, giving device compatibilities for all recent versions of Windows including Windows XP.

Device Manager

If an existing device isn't working properly in Windows XP, it's time to check out its listing in Device Manager. Go to Start, Control Panel, Printers and other hardware, then click on System in the left-hand pane. This brings up the System Properties dialog. Choose the Hardware tab and click on Device Manager. This

shows a list of your system devices in a hierarchical tree structure. Expand each branch by clicking on the plus signs. Any device showing a yellow exclamation mark has driver difficulties.

To see driver details for a device, double click its entry in device manager. This shows the Properties dialog. From here you can see details about the device, update its driver, alter its resource use, roll the driver back to a previous one or disable the device.

Finding new drivers

To find new drivers, your first point of call should be Windows Update. Choose Start, All Programs, and Windows Update. The computer connects to the internet and goes to the Microsoft Windows Update website. The site interrogates your computer and looks for updates to Windows and for approved device drivers. Once the scan is complete, you can choose to install any of the updates you like.

The suggested device drivers should be fine to install, as they will definitely be approved as compatible with Windows XP. The download can take several minutes or somewhat longer, so be patient. The updates will install themselves and then ask you to restart your computer.

If Windows Update doesn't provide you with a suitable driver, your next port of call is the website of the company that created the device. Look to see if they have recently developed a Windows XP compatible driver. If there is no sign of one, email their support address and ask if they plan to develop one. If all sources of investigation come up with a blank, you may need to try out a driver that is not specifically supported by Windows XP. Microsoft will not be able to support you if you decide to go down this route.

If you have updated a driver and then found that the device no longer works, Windows XP lets you roll the driver back to its previous state. Do this from the device's Driver tab in Device Manager.

Use the Device Manager to solve hardware and driver installation problems

Navigating the Device Driver installer

1. General Tab
This gives general information about the device, what it is, if it is working properly and its location. You can use a troubleshooting wizard from here or disable the device.

2. Properties tab
More info about the device, including what other devices it interacts with.

3. Driver tab
Full information about the driver, including its compatibility signature.

4. Resources Tab
Informs you of the technical resources the device uses, including any conflicts.

5. Driver Details button
Gives full details of all files the driver uses and their location on your computer.

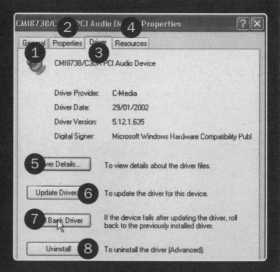

6. Update Driver button
Lets you install an updated driver from CD, floppy disk or over the internet.

7. Roll Back Driver button
Allows you to return to an

earlier version of the driver if an update has been unsuccessful.

8. Uninstall button
Press this button to remove the driver from your system.

Device Manager, it has either not been physically installed properly, or it is not Windows XP compatible.

If it appears in Device Manager and the driver is properly installed, but it still won't work, it is likely that you have two or more devices that conflict, i.e. they try to use the same system resources at the same time. You can resolve this by moving the device to a different socket, if there is another available.

Don't panic!
If this still doesn't resolve your problem, the conflict can still be resolved. However, it's time to call in the experts to sort it out.

If all this sounds like Windows XP is

too complicated for you, remember that most of this goes on in the background and you needn't worry about it.

The only time you need explore the features mentioned here within this article, is when things don't quite work as they should. Thankfully, Windows XP sees to it that such times are few and far between. ■

Jargon

■ Driver
A program that tells Windows XP how to control a device that's connected to your computer.

Clean machine!
Using Scheduled Tasks

You don't need to remember to download the latest utilities and virus definitions to keep your PC in tip-top shape. Just set your system up so it happens automatically

Just as buying a burglar alarm but not fitting it won't protect your house, the maintenance tools in Windows XP can't keep your PC running smoothly if you never get around to using them.

If you remember to scan your system for viruses and download the latest virus updates regularly, you're far less likely to get caught out by the latest attack. And if you back up your files regularly, deleting files by accident or losing them to a virus will be annoying rather than a disaster.

The trouble is most of us can't be bothered until it's too late. Luckily, Windows XP has the solution – a way of automating all these tasks so you don't need to spend time on them.

Starting up

The simplest way to run a utility automatically is to put it in the Startup folder in the All Programs section of the Start menu; that way it will run whenever you switch on your PC.

But adding tools like Backup and Disk Defragment to Startup isn't the most flexible way to work. For instance, if you put your PC on standby rather than shutting down, it may be weeks before you start your PC from scratch. And doing maintenance jobs right at the start of your day may not be the best time.

Scheduling tasks

Instead, use the Scheduled Tasks control panel to run tools at a convenient time. This control panel shows which tasks are already scheduled but it also includes an Add Scheduled Task wizard. Adding new tasks is very simple with the wizard but you can get more timing options if you do it manually.

Just right-click on any task and choose Properties (or tick the box marked 'Open advanced properties for this task when I click Finish' on the last page of the wizard).

You can schedule tasks depending on how you use your PC: as well as running a task when you start your PC or when you log on, you can pick 'When Idle' to have the task run whenever your PC isn't busy. You can also set an end date, if you only want to run the task for a month.

From the Settings pane you can control how the task runs. To stop a task running indefinitely you can force it to stop after a certain amount of time. You can also make sure tasks that will slow the system down don't run when you're busy.

If you want the task to stop as soon as you start using your PC, tick 'Stop the task if the computer ceases to be idle'. If you leave your PC in Standby mode, set it to wake up in the middle of the night, and do the long slow maintenance task when it least interferes with your work.

Adding tasks manually

If you know you'll need to change a lot of settings you can skip the wizard interface completely: choose File, New, Scheduled Task to get a blank task that defaults to 9am and use the Properties dialog to fill in the details. If you want to try the task out straight away, rather than waiting till it runs automatically to see if it works properly, right-click on it and choose Run.

You can delete a task, but if you just want to stop it running for a while then open the Properties dialog and untick Enable on the Task tab.

Setting the time

When you set the time for maintenance tasks, work out whether you need to be there when they run. Defragmenting your disk and backing up files are best run when you're not using your PC, so that all the files are available. Running a disk scan to check for potential problems with your drive can take an hour and will slow your system down, so it's best done when you don't have to wait for it. Other tools need you there to respond to messages, so you'll want to schedule checking Windows Update or scanning the Registry for out-of-date keys for when you're around.

Check the log to see that the jobs you are running when you're not around have run without any errors. Alternatively, choose Advanced, Notify Me of Missed Tasks to see a warning on screen: if you keep seeing warnings for the same missed task, change the scheduled time so that it runs immediately and then pick a new regular time. ■

≫ Planning your maintenance

Scheduling events means you won't forget to do them

DAILY

1.Check for anti-virus updates
It may sound paranoid, but it only takes a day for a new virus to spread like wildfire, so if you use the Internet every day, take just a few minutes to check for new virus definitions. Most anti-virus software will check automatically – Norton AntiVirus looks for new definitions every four hours if you're online – but make sure you switch the feature on. If your software doesn't check, put a task into the Windows Scheduler, or make the update site the home page in your browser.

2.Backup
Depending on how much you use your PC, you may want to back up daily or weekly. A good rule of thumb is to do a backup for every eight hours you use the PC.

WEEKLY

1.Anti-virus sweep
Run a full scan of your system at least once a week. Even though good anti-virus software checks every file you download or open, you could get infected with a virus before the software gets the details of the new virus. You wouldn't know the virus was there until you opened the file again or it started causing problems.

2.Defragment
If you create and delete a lot of files and install new software regularly, you'll want to defragment your drive every week; if you don't use the PC as much, once a month should do. If you want to keep an eye on your drive you can analyse the disk while you're working on your PC to see how badly it's fragmented, but it's best to run the defrag when you don't have any files open.

3.Delete temp files
Whether you do it by hand or use the Disk Cleanup tool, get rid of old temporary files, including temporary Internet files, and empty the Recycle Bin. Delete these before you defragment your hard drive: there's no point spending time juggling files you're not going to keep and they'll leave more space for the defrag utility.

MONTHLY

1.Look for new drivers
If you've got Windows Update set to download automatically (or to alert you to new updates) you'll get critical updates, but you'll have to check for new drivers by hand. Look on Windows Update and on the manufacturers' Web sites.

2.Backup
If you're doing a full backup of your system, do a new one every month so you don't have to keep a lot of smaller backups around. If you've added new hardware, make a new system recovery disk.

3.Clean the Registry
Use a utility like RegCleaner (www.jv16.org) or Norton CleanSweep to get rid of out of date Registry keys.

4.Clean your computer
Unfortunately, you can't get Windows XP to do this for you, but you'll want to clean your screen (use an antistatic wipe if you can), turn your keyboard upside down and shake it to dislodge crumbs and dust (and dust underneath it), give your mouse a clean (even optical mice pick up grime and dust on the glides) and make sure that your PC's fan isn't clogged with dust. Do this regularly and you'll increase the life of your PC.

Getting started with Broadband ADSL

Other web users are whizzing past you on the fast lane, downloading files, watching films online and playing games over the internet. Isn't it time you joined them?

Over the last two months, 'Broadband' has hit the news. With Cable and ADSL (the two main broadband technologies) getting involved in a price war, the cost of broadband is at an all-time low. The drop in prices has been triggered by BT cost-cutting and also by the launch of self-install broadband so you don't need an engineer to come and install a modem.

On April 1st 2002, BT Wholesale, BT's broadband arm that sells services to ISPs, reduced the price each ISP must pay for an ADSL connection from £25 to £14.75 per month. By slashing subscription costs, the price of ADSL has almost halved in the past few months and more and more people are now asking what broadband can do for them.

We could start by giving you a technical definition of what broadband is, but you don't have to know how something works to use it.

The bottom line is that broadband works, it's likely to be ten times faster than your current internet connection and it is now available for less than 80p a day.

Before we go any further, it's best to find out whether or not you can actually connect to a broadband operator. Depending on where you live you may be able to receive ADSL, cable or both. If your area is not covered yet, you could be in for a wait as broadband is currently in a period of consolidation and new areas won't be covered for a while.

Cable-based internet connections are only available to about 25 per cent of the population, and although the pricing is competitive, the likelihood is that you'll

>> Making sure you are secure

A firewall is even more vital if you are using 'always on' broadband

One of the most important issues you must address once you have decided to purchase a broadband connection is security. A recent survey from security experts Symantec found that 95% of home internet users surveyed in the UK were subject to an attack.

Symantec surveyed 167 users over a period of a month and not only found that 95% of users were attacked but that each received an average of 56 intrusion attempts every day. The majority of these home users were on 56k modems so you can imagine the risk of having an unprotected 'always on' broadband machine at the mercy of hackers. Thankfully you won't have to spend hundreds of pounds to secure your PC as Windows XP comes with its own Internet Connection Firewall. There's also a firewall on our disc and a great utility called ZoneAlarm that can be downloaded for free at: www.zonealarm.com/zap26_za_grid.html.

have to opt for an ADSL service. ADSL is only available on BT phone lines, and will theoretically work for about 70 per cent of the country's subscribers.

Deciding which ADSL package you're going to opt for is a complicated affair. Not only do you need to take monthly subscription costs into account but also the cost of installation (which is free with some self-install packages) and the cost of a modem (around £100) which can be bought from the broadband provider or independently. To compare the ADSL services available, go to www.adslguide.org.uk/isp_compare.asp.

There are currently around 200,000 cable customers and 160,000 using ADSL in the UK. Prior to recent price cuts, BT Wholesale were receiving 3,000 orders a week but following the price cuts this figure has now more than doubled.

So, broadband is out there, it's cheaper than ever and available to the majority of the country, but what's the point? Well, anyone that plays games online, wants to download music in a matter of minutes not hours, or has longed for the day they can stream quality video via their internet connection will see broadband as a godsend and it will revolutionise their internet experience.

Good or bad?
However, there have been some horror stories. People have had problems getting connected, been unable to get through on support lines and been left waiting for weeks in between visits from engineers. Thanks to the self-install packages now available you can cut out the middle-man and greatly reduce the possibility of problems with your broadband connection. If you need to call a tech support line during peak times, the likelihood is you'll be waiting a while before you get through.

To find out how easy it is to subscribe to an ADSL provider, we decided to give it a go. We went to www.adslguide.org.uk for the latest prices and packages and found a self-install option offering free set-up for the first few thousand customers with a monthly subscription cost of under £25.

Having signed up at the website we received a confirmation email informing us that our information had been passed on to BT (this will happen whichever ADSL provider you sign up with) and were informed BT would then carry out line checks and activate ADSL on our line. We decided to buy our modem (an Alcatel Speed Touch USB) from the ISP for £99 (the RRP for which is around £120).

The modem arrived the next day. First we installed the drivers on a Windows XP machine. Then we had to connect a micro filter to the phone socket – this Is placed on the socket to separate voice and data traffic so you can still make and receive calls while online. This filter has two sockets, one for your phone and one for your modem. The last thing you have to do once connecting your phone and modem correctly is re-start your PC plugging the modem into your USB port. Now we just needed to wait for our line to be enabled. Most ISPs quote a seven day waiting period before BT connects you but we only had to wait four days before our modem began to work

Now it was time to see just how quick broadband really is. Although many describe ADSL as 'always on' it is still a session-based technology and you still have to sign in. However this takes seconds rather than minutes once you have logged on. You will notice the difference between your 56k modem and your new ADSL connection immediately. Web pages pop straight into your browser, music appears in seconds and movies stream at an awesome rate.

You can test the speed of your new connection by going to www.dslreports.com/stest/0 – ours was consistently high, but there was a slight drop off at peak times.

In the coming months major ISPs will be launching 'out of the box' solutions that will be available from major PC retailers and will make it even easier to get connected – but why wait? If you can plug in a modem and wait a few days there's nothing stopping you joining the broadband revolution now. ∎

Hosting a website

Your website could be the most entertaining and informative one around, but if it's not online, it won't be seen. We take you on a quick tour of the hidden world of web hosting...

So, you've finished your killer website and the world is waiting to be amazed by your design skills and wit. There's one problem – your site is stuck on your PC where no-one can see it. What do you do?

Well, the answer is simple; all you need do is place your site somewhere where other people's computers can come and grab it to download to their own machine. Enter the wonderful world of hosting.

The problem is that most people view hosting as a massively complicated affair, when, at its basic level, it really isn't.

Behind the doors of your web host you'll find hundreds of servers, merely glorified storage devices, each packed with personal and corporate websites ready to be found.

But before you dive in, there are certain key points you need to know.

First things first then – who should I get to host my website? This is where things get a little more complicated as there are literally hundreds of choices out there. For beginners and those just wanting a basic website with pictures of you and your family there are plenty of pay-as-you go ISPs offering the minimum in services and support. When you sign up you can get, in most cases, a limited amount of web hosting space. www.tiscali.co.uk, for example, offers 50MB of free web space to house your website. However, free ISPs do have their limitations.

Most won't allow you to include flashy additions to your website such as streaming media and many pepper your lovingly created

≫ Frontpage hosting and msn communities

There are websites to suit all ambitions and budgets

If you use Microsoft FrontPage 2000 or 2002 to create your site, make sure that your host supports FrontPage extensions. These are the special commands you need to include special add-ons such as discussion groups, text searches and surveys.

Your host will let you know what you have to do to activate your FrontPage extensions, although this is mostly just a case of selecting checkboxes on your domain's online control panel.

MSN Communities

If all this sounds too complicated or expensive for you, you could consider creating an MSN community. This is a website set up for a number of people to share views, pictures and chat on a specific subject. However, once you've created a community, there is an option to create an extremely basic website, hosted for free by MSN and allowing you to add text, tables or pictures. Just remember community hosted websites aren't

known for their style or class. To have a go, point your browser at http://communities.msn.co.uk/home, create a community by answering the questions and then add a web page via the 'Add a Page to Your Community' option in your manager tools. It's then just a case of formatting your text or selecting pictures from your computer for upload.

European hosts: Tiscali offer a range of hosting deals including free web space

web pages with banner advertising, which can be annoying for visitors.

Plus, your web address will also include the ISP's name, OK for small home pages but hardly the most professional or slick image to portray, especially if you are building a site for your business.

There are ways around this last problem with free services such as www.v3.com which offers shorter names along the lines of http://go.to/yourname but again, for a more professional look you should think about buying your own domain name. More of that later.

Shared Hosting

Where should you go next, then, if you want something more from your site? Most small websites can opt for Shared Hosting, a paid for service that usually gives you a unique domain name as well as a POP3 email address and a larger amount of available web space.

The price you pay can also rely on what kind of domain name you're after. There are a whole host (if you excuse the pun) of

domain names out there ranging from localised domains such as .co.uk (for websites found in the UK) to new classifications such as .name, ideal for individuals. The most common domain, .com, is in shorter supply and largely also more expensive.

It's here that we also encounter yet another important element of hosting; download bandwidth. When you sign on, your host will let you know an amount of data that they will allow to be transferred from your site. Be warned though; go beyond that figure and you could find your website frozen, although most hosts warn you via email if you're reaching your limit.

Choosing a host

There are certain things you should ask any potential host before signing on the dotted line. First of all, check its stability. Hosts come and go at an alarming rate so you should check on its history and find out if it's profitable, otherwise you could be courting a host that will vanish within a few weeks or months.

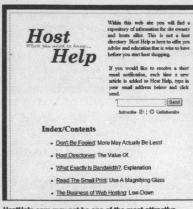

Host Help

When you work in house...

Within this web site you will find a repository of information for site owners and hosts alike. This is not a host directory. Host Help is here to offer you advise and education that is wise to have before you start host shopping.

If you would like to receive a short email notification, each time a new article is added to Host Help, type in your email address below and click send.

[   ] [Send]

Subscribe ⊙ | ○ UnSubscribe

Index/Contents

- Don't Be Fooled: More May Actually Be Less!
- Host Directories: The Value Of...
- What Exactly Is Bandwidth?: Explanation
- Read The Small Print: Use A Magnifying Glass
- The Business of Web Hosting: Low-Down

HostHelp.com may not be one of the most attractive websites, but it's full of useful info on how to find a host

Also make sure that your host is compatible with Windows XP. Are they Windows based? Can they cope with Frontpage extensions? You also need to find out what support is available if something goes wrong. Are there people standing by on the phones (and if so, do you have to pay through the nose for expensive call charges?) and when is the helpdesk open. Some hosts offer 24-7 support service while others rely on email responses. Work out how much support you think you will need and how important it is that your site is up and running at all times.

One of the main reasons for contacting your host is when you discover that your website has suddenly become unavailable.

Jargon

■ Server
The physical computer that holds all your Web pages. It is assigned an IP address that allows users to log on and download your site.

■ FTP
File Transfer Protocol, a method of sending files over the Internet. Many hosts use this as a way of receiving your website files.

Ask your host what uptime it boasts – the amount of time it can guarantee that your website will be available for viewing. Most offer 99 per cent, as there will always be some time of unavailability due to technical problems or maintenance. Be wary of anything less than that however, especially if you are creating a site for your business. Visitors that come to your site to find it unavailable may never return. Remember, your competitors are a mere mouse click away.

The final major concern with hosting is security. With viruses and hacking on the increase you should check that your host has a good firewall, a barrier that stops harmful content or criminals breaking into or infecting your data. The need for security increases one hundred-fold if you're thinking about selling online or receiving customers' credit card details, but in these cases its best to go for special secure hosting deals.

Uploading

Once you've chosen your host, you obviously have to know how to get your website onto their servers so browsers can see it. Most hosts use FTP (File Transfer Protocol) methods which can be accessed via a program such as cuteFTP. You will be given an ftp address (much like an http:// address but with FTP at the front) and a password to gain access. Once it's all connected it's just a case of dragging the files from your PC to the host's server for uploading.

It's even easier if you are using FrontPage 2000 or 2002 to publish your site. All you need to do is go to the Publish Web command from the File Menu and enter the web address that you're publishing your site to, along with a login name and password that your Host will give you. FrontPage does the rest. However, publishing your site this way means that your host needs to have certain compatible elements. Another thing to ask your host!

Above all, choosing the right host is all about working out exactly what you want and finding the best match. Before you get out your credit card, sit down and work out what you want to do with your website and then spend some time shopping around. ■

Finding new fonts

How you use fonts depends partly on the image you want to present. Here's where to find the coolest fonts and how to set up Windows XP to use them

You use fonts every day on your computer, when you type a letter or even when you're viewing a website. You already have lots of fonts on your PC, but what exactly is a font and how are they used, and can you get more?

A font is a collection of characters (0-9, a-z, A-Z, punctuation and other sundry characters) which all have the same design. Each font has a name, for example Arial or Times New Roman and most can be produced in an almost infinite range of sizes.

Many of the fonts you have were installed with Windows XP, others may have come with programs you have installed. Programs likely to include fonts are Microsoft Office, publishing and graphics software.

Once a font is installed by any program, it is automatically available for you to use elsewhere.

Some fonts are special – for example, the system fonts which Windows uses – and others form part of a collection of fonts known as the Web Core fonts. Most, however, are there simply for you to use.

Getting new fonts

You can buy or download additional fonts for your PC. You can buy font collections at any high street computer store or you can find fonts on the web.

Many fonts on the web are free for download, others are shareware or available for purchase.

Type "free fonts" into your favourite search engine to see just how popular fonts are and how many font download sites there are.

One such site is Font Mania at www.webfxmall.com/fonts, which has a good array of easily viewed fonts.

Another fun site is Famous fonts which has fonts from the movies, TV, advertising and sports (www.eliteentertainment.net/famousfonts/).

Be aware that it is possible to have too

Using the features

- ClearType smooths the edges of the fonts in Windows XP making them easier to read

- Turn ClearType on and off via the Effects button in Display Properties/Appearance

- Boost the size at which Windows XP displays fonts (useful if you are visually impaired) via the Font size box in Display Properties/Appearance

More information

How to tune ClearType
- You can tune the way Windows XP displays ClearType fonts at www.microsoft.com/typography/cleartype/cleartypeactivate.htm.

Just view the text that is shown and select the example which looks best to you. Windows XP will then alter the way the font is displayed on your screen, to your preference.

Jargon

■ Web Core fonts
These are fonts which are free for download and accepted for use on the web as most people have them installed and can see them.

■ Find more about these at www.microsoft.com/typography/fontpack

many fonts and some programs will function erratically or give error messages when you have more than 500 fonts installed on your machine.

ClearType

ClearType is a new feature in Windows XP which improves the clarity of type on certain monitors: in particular, laptops and flat screen LCD monitors. It works by using extra coloured pixels to smooth the edges of letters.

It is up to you whether you enable ClearType. If you're using a standard CRT monitor you may not see any improvement and the effect may even make your text look rather hazy.

To enable ClearType, right-click on your desktop, choose Properties, Appearance, Effects. Enable the 'Use the following method to smooth the edges of screen fonts' box and choose ClearType from the drop-down list.

Take a look on the previous page where we show how you can tune ClearType via the Web. ■

STEP BY STEP

⟩⟩ Downloading and installing new fonts

So you've found a cool font online – now download and install it for use

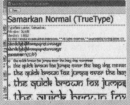

1 **CHOOSE YOUR FONT**
Follow the font site's procedure for downloading. On Font Mania you click the font sample to start the font download. When the File Download dialog displays, click Save then, when the Save As dialog appears select the folder to store the file in – or create a new folder called 'Downloaded fonts to use'.

2 **EXTRACT AND ENABLE**
When 'Download complete' appears, if the font is a Zip file (.zip), click Open to open the zip file and choose Extract and extract the .ttf file to your folder. If not, click Close. Choose Start, Control Panel, Fonts then choose File, Install New Font. Find the font file, tick 'Copy to Fonts folder' checkbox, then

3 **VIEW YOUR NEW FONT**
View your new font by locating its icon and click it to open a sampler page displaying the font. Click Print to print a sample. This Fonts area is where you remove fonts too: right-click it and choose Delete. Once the font is installed it will be available in the font list of every Windows program.

Getting more from ZIP files

Organise your hard drive and conserve valuable space for your latest software – in less time than it took to read this sentence

The average modern PC comes with at least 40 gigabytes worth of hard disk space to play with. Initially, this seems almost ludicrously big: just compare it with a 1.4MB floppy disk, or even the 650MB that's sufficient to hold almost any application on a CD. Don't expect this feeling to last.

If you play a lot of games or use powerful packages such as Microsoft Office XP, the space quickly drips away – and that's before you consider documents, settings and the other files that make your PC work.

It's worth thinking now about how to conserve space; of the methods available to you, none is cheaper or more efficient than Zipped Folders.

You've almost certainly used these already without realising it. You may have a .ZIP file on your hard disk; failing that, it's the format that most applications on the internet use in order to keep file downloads small.

Working it

Place a .ZIP file on your Desktop and double-click it – note that it acts much like any other folder.

The difference is that the files you're now looking at have been crushed to take up as little space as possible on your hard drive.

You can interact with these files just like any others: drag and drop new ones in, copy them to other parts of your computer on their own, or use the whole

archive at once. As you can see, it requires no effort.

The one exception is if you try to run an executable file ('setup.exe', say), in which case Windows XP will have to copy the files out of the folder to ensure that it can find them all. In this case, simply follow the on-screen instructions – the default option will place them in a brand new folder located on your Desktop.

Creating an archive

Let's go a step further and create an archive. Select the files you want to compress with the mouse. Once highlighted, right-click on them, select the

Installing WinZip

■ If you decide to install a standalone compression program, such as WinZip, this program's name and icon will replace 'Compressed (Zipped) Folders' in the right-click menu.

Jargon

■ Archive
Another name for the Zipped Folders in Windows XP.

■ Encryption
The process of scrambling a file so that only you can read its contents.

More information

Windows XP Home Edition Product Documentation

■ www.microsoft.com/windowsxp/home/using/productdoc

Send To menu and finally 'Compressed (Zipped) Folder', then wait a few seconds for the new archive to appear on screen. Double-click to open it and see the contained files.

Encryption

Zipped folders offer one further tool – encryption. To protect a set of files from prying eyes, you can assign the folder a password.

Open the Zipped Folder we just created and right-click on the white background. Select Add A Password from the menu.

You have to enter your password twice so you don't inadvertently lock yourself out. Be creative when picking real passwords, preferably using a mix of letters and numbers.

To unprotect the files, just right-click on it again and select the Remove Password option from the menu.

There's a collection of Zip file utilities you can download online – we recommend Zip Genius and BXAutoZip. ■

STEP BY STEP

≫ Zipping and encrypting your folders

Zipped Folders are deceptively easy to use – here's how...

1 ZIPPED FOLDERS
Zipped Folders are almost identical to the conventional kind, with just two distinguishing features: a zipper on the folder icon, and the Extract All Files command under Folder Tasks. You can use any file contained in a Zipped Folder as you would any other on your hard drive, editing, copying and deleting files as required.

2 CHOOSE A PASSWORD
Right-click and select Add a Password to protect your data. When choosing one, be careful: your own name, that of your pets, favourite sports teams and other such trivia are easy to guess. The best password consists of a mix of numbers and letters – but don't make it so complicated that you can't remember it yourself...

3 EXTRACTING FILES
Running many executable files or selecting Extract All Files will load this wizard. This will copy files from a Zipped Folder to elsewhere on your drive. It is also capable of creating new folders if none of your existing ones is available – but bear in mind that it will also ask for a password if the data is protected.

Speed up your CDs

Copy a CD into a folder, assign the folder a drive letter and gain a big speed boost. Here's how

How many CD ROMs do you have cluttering up the place? Chances are you have quite a few – but you may be surprised how little you use them. CD ROMs have been superseded by DVDs in the amount of data they can hold and, compared to your hard drive, their access speed is sluggish.

While most software is still supplied on a humble CD, it's really designed to sit in your drive only during installation. With a few exceptions, the days of programs that require a CD to be permanently inserted are pretty much gone. 650MB is no longer the enormous size that it seemed during the CD's heyday: most hard drives are 50 times as big or larger. With the Internet fast becoming the ultimate reference tool, it's easy to see why CD ROMs aren't as popular as they once were.

Essential CDs

Despite this, you may well have a copy of Microsoft Encarta or other reference works on CD. They are still useful, if a little inconvenient, given the need to swap

Use Windows Media Player to copy audio CDs to compressed files on your hard drive

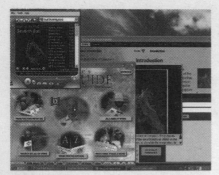

With Virtual CDs you can run several CD ROMs at once or listen to an audio CD, all without using your CD drive

discs and the slow access, not to mention the noise created by the faster CD drives. If you could access your CDs by just following a Start menu or desktop shortcut, they could again find a use.

Achieving this may not be difficult; it depends on the age and complexity of your CD. One way to do this is to simply copy the data from your CD to a folder on your hard drive. Once copied, you can install the CD from its new location.

Amazingly, in some cases this works perfectly well. In some instances, however, these copied CDs need to have their own drive letters assigned to them.

This is a little trickier to pull off. You could try using a partitioning tool, which divides your hard drive into a number of smaller, logical drives. Windows XP treats logical drives as if they were discrete hard drives of fixed size. Software like Partition Magic 7 will let you do this without destroying any data on your hard disk, but it is rather like using a sledge hammer to crack a nut. You would end up with a number of hard drives, each 650MB big.

A far better idea is to copy the contents of your CD to a folder on your hard disk, then persuade Windows XP to treat this folder as a separate drive. You could add or remove data from the folder, or even delete it completely, without upsetting Windows XP.

Windows XP contains a command that will enable you to do precisely this. It's called subst.exe and it lurks in the depths of the System32 folder. Running subst.exe with the correct parameters will map a drive letter to any folder you like.

STEP BY STEP

≫ Copying the CD onto your hard drive

Start by copying the contents of your CD to a folder on your hard drive

1 LOAD THE CD
Put your CD into your CD drive, holding down Shift to stop it running automatically. Click Start, My Computer. Right click on your CD ROM drive and choose Explore in order to view its contents in a brand new Windows Explorer window.

2 SELECT ALL FILES
Click on Edit, Select All. This highlights all the CD's contents. Now choose Edit, Copy to folder. Browse to the place you want to put the files and click Make New Folder. Now you can right click on the new folder and rename it Virtual.

3 COPY THE FILES
Click Copy. The files from your CD are now copied to this folder on your hard drive. This takes several minutes, depending on the speed of your CD drive. If your CD is a simple one, you may be able to install from this folder with no other alteration.

STEP BY STEP

>> Mapping a virtual drive

Use subst.exe to map a virtual drive every time you run Windows XP

1 CREATE A SHORTCUT
Right click anywhere on the desktop and choose New, Shortcut. In the Create Shortcut dialog, enter the path 'C:\WINDOWS\SYSTEM32\subst.exe h: C:\[virtual]', where 'C:\[virtual]' is the folder you copied your CD data to and H: is the drive going to be mapped.

2 CHOOSE AN ICON
Click Next and Finish. Now right click on your new shortcut and choose Properties from the menu. Click on Change Icon and choose an icon from the list. It's best to choose something that will remind you what the shortcut does, so choose a CD icon. Click Apply.

3 ADD IT TO STARTUP
Click on Start, My Computer. Double click on your hard drive, Open Documents and Settings, All Users, Start Menu, Programs, Startup. Drag your shortcut from the desktop to the Startup folder. Now restart your PC. You should have a new hard drive, with the drive letter H.

Assigning a drive

You now need to make sure that the drive letter is mapped to this folder each time Windows starts. This means putting a shortcut to the subst.exe utility into the Startup folder for all users. Make a shortcut by right clicking anywhere on the desktop and choosing New, Shortcut. Click on Browse to locate subst.exe. You'll find it in WINDOWS\SYSTEM32.

Alternatively, type the path 'C:\WINDOWS\SYSTEM32\subst.exe H: C:\[virtual]', where H: is the drive letter you want to map and 'C:\[virtual]' is the folder containing your CD files.

Browse to C:\Documents and Settings\All Users\Start Menu\Programs\Startup, and drag your newly created shortcut into this folder.

Virtual CD software

It's worth noting that some CDs are written so they'll only run from a CD drive, and simply giving them a drive letter won't work. This gives the CDs copy protection, but it can be slightly irritating if all you want to do is make your own copy more convenient to use. For CDs of this type, you'll need to get some software that will generate a virtual CD drive, so that Windows XP not only gives the drive a letter, but recognises it as a genuine CD drive during use. Virtual CD and Virtual Drive Personal are two applications you'll find helpful for this.

So how can you be sure which CDs work and which ones won't? The only way to be sure is to have a go, although most versions of Encarta will run quite happily from your hard drive. ■

Jargon

■ Partition
A section of a hard drive that Windows XP treats as a completely separate drive. There are several programs available that can create partitions, the most popular being Partition Magic. It's difficult to reverse any partitioning, so it's only recommended if you know what you are doing.

Animated wallpaper!

Take one HTML file, add a dash of video and you've got the recipe for an amazing animated desktop – and you can add even more interactive features later

The idea of a desktop background you can interact with has been a distinctive feature in Microsoft Windows for several years. It first made an appearance when Windows 95 was launched, and was one of its most innovative new features, bringing with it new levels of customisation.

Rather than having a plain image as your wallpaper, the Active Desktop gave you the opportunity to make your backdrops much more interesting by using a Web page instead.

Although it's no longer referred to as the Active Desktop, the feature is still very much a part of the Display Properties in Windows XP. Anything from your favourite Web site to your personal home page can be used, the only criterion being that it's a HTML file you use. Bear in mind HTML files can be accessed from your hard drive as well as the Internet, and a world of possibilities opens up. All that's required is a little imagination.

Use movie files

If you were asked to think of all the file types that could be incorporated into a Web page to create a display with impact, you would probably come up with the likes

---

STEP BY STEP

>> Getting started

The first thing you need to do is incorporate your movie into a Web page

1 ASSEMBLE THE ELEMENTS
The first thing to do is create a folder to store all the elements of your Web page: for example, the HTML file, the bliss.avi file (download this from www.microsoft.com/windowsxp/pro/downloads/bliss.asp). We suggest storing the folder under My Documents and calling it

2 START YOUR WEB PAGE
The next stage is to create the HTML. If you have no prior knowledge of Web page coding, you'll need to use an HTML editor or Web page creation program. We'll be using Microsoft FrontPage 2002 for this tutorial. Create a new Web page and save it as desktop.htm.

3 ADD THE MOVIE
Now we need to incorporate the bliss.avi file into our new page. In Microsoft FrontPage 2002, click on Insert, Picture, Video, select the file bliss.avi from the folder My Documents\ DeskPage and click on Open. This will display a static preview in FrontPage, rather than a moving image.

>> Editing your web page code

A few adjustments are needed to make the movie fit your PC display

1 VIEW YOUR HTML CODE
Click on the HTML tab underneath the image in order to view the coding that goes into making up the page. Go down to the paragraph tag <p>, where you'll see the filename bliss.avi along with the command to open the file and a setting in pixels for the dimensions of the movie.

2 LOOP THE VIDEO FILE
At the moment our video file will play only once, then stop. In order to give it a more natural effect as if it were a real landscape, we need to make it play constantly. To do this, we need to add an extra piece of code after "fileopen" as follows: loop="infinite".

3 ADJUST TO FIT
The movie width and height settings need to match your display settings, otherwise your AVI won't fit the display correctly. If you're running your display at 1,024 x 768, for example, amend these two figures accordingly. Save the changes, then close desktop.htm and FrontPage 2002.

of .gif, .jpg, and .png – all static image formats. But there's one file type that can create an even greater impression on a Web page: the AVI movie file. Movie clips are not used on the Internet too often because of large file sizes and bandwidth considerations.

However, we already know that an HTML file can be run from your hard drive, so there's nothing to stop you incorporating an AVI movie file in a Web page on your hard drive, then using it in your very own desktop.

Choosing a file

You've probably seen the Bliss background image under Display Properties, which forms part of the standard Windows XP theme with its green rolling hills, beautiful blue sky and wispy white clouds.

With that static image turned into an AVI movie file and incorporated into a Web page, you're on your way to creating a truly stunning desktop. You can download a copy of the file from www.microsoft.com/windowsxp/pro/downloads/bliss.asp:

>> Streaming webcam footage to your desktop

How to add live video, stock tickers and more

Now that you know how to add Web content to your desktop, you can start having some fun. As well as AVIs, there are many other elements you can use within your Web page. Here are a few ideas you can use to get you started.

EarthCam (www.earthcam.com) is a great way to get a Web cam view on your desktop, with everything from Space Shuttle launches to global landmarks including the Eiffel Tower and Red Square, Moscow.

WebCam Central (www.camcentral.com) offers more great Web cams including the Panda, Gorilla and Africa cams.

The Internet Explorer Desktop Gallery (www.microsoft.com/windows/ie/previous/gallery/default.asp) is designed primarily for an older version of the Web browser, but you can still make use of ideas like an investor ticker, up to the minute sports news and a satellite tracking map.

STEP BY STEP

>> Select your web page

Your Web page is now ready to view as your desktop

  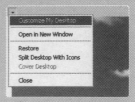

1 **ACTIVATE THE DESKTOP**
You now need to locate your Web page. Right click on the desktop and choose Properties. Select the Desktop tab, click on Customize Desktop and select the Web tab. Click on New followed by Browse and locate your desktop.htm file. Click Open then OK.

2 **TEST YOUR WEB PAGE**
Under the list of Web Pages you'll see that your file is checked: click on OK, then click on Apply, followed by OK again. The bliss.avi file will now start playing on your desktop. If it doesn't fill the whole screen, drag it from the corners and sides to fit.

3 **ACCESSING PROPERTIES**
Because your desktop image is now a Web page, the normal right click functions won't appear when you try them. To access the Display Properties again, move the cursor to the top left of the page and click on Customize Desktop.

Now all that's left for you to do is create the HTML page and start using it in Windows XP. Our step by step guide will provide you with full details on how you can achieve this incredible effect on your own site.

Once you've grasped the principle of placing an AVI file within a Web page, there's no end to the possibilities.

You may have captured some great footage on your digital video camera, so why not take a clip and use it on your desktop? Then there's your favourite moment from a movie, or your team scoring that last minute winning goal.

Desktop TV

Anyone fortunate enough to have broadband, in the form of ADSL or cable, will be able to exploit the high speed connection they now have.

There are plenty of Web sites that offer live Web casts using streamed video.

You could create a Web page containing links to such broadcasts, and have them displaying as your desktop background.

Something else you could try is a Web page that contains links to your favourite MP3 and WMA files, and has them play automatically from your desktop or when selected by other users. ■

Speed up Windows XP

50 Windows XP speed-up tips

Everyone can do with a boost – and thanks to Windows XP, there's more than one way to get it. Whether it's saving time or going faster, there's stacks you can do right now

Everyone uses their PC differently, so default settings in Windows XP are designed for ease of use rather than performance. Not all these tips are for beginners, so if you are new to the Registry, for example, it's best to avoid it. If not, remember to back it up.

Clean hard drive
The more disk space you have free, the faster your PC can run: there's space to defragment files and to use for virtual memory. Keep at least 700MB free.

Run Disk Cleanup
Run this utility from the System Tools menu to clear internet cache files, temporary files and other clutter.

Clear System Restore Points
Making System Restore Points automatically can soon fill up your hard drive. When your PC is working well, open System Restore and pick System Restore Settings. Now tick 'Turn off System Restore on all Drives' and tick Apply to delete all old Restore Points, then create one manually.

Fix virtual memory
Set the paging file for virtual memory to a fixed size: it's less likely to slow down your system. Check the memory your applications need in Total Commit Charge in Task Manager's Performance tab, and add 32MB.

In System Properties' Advanced tab, choose Performance, Settings, Advanced and click Change under Virtual Memory. Change the Paging file size to Custom size, with the Initial and Maximum size the same. Don't make the figure smaller than what's currently allocated.

Turn off other users

If other users on your PC leave applications running when they're away, it slows you down. If you can't log in under their names to close programs, use Logoff in Task Manager's Users tab to shut them down; they'll lose any unsaved files.

Turn off effects

Windows XP picks the visual effects it thinks your PC can handle, but you can turn off menu transitions, shadows and font smoothing if you prefer. Click Effects in the Appearance tab of the Display Properties Control Panel and experiment.

Turn off effects 2

More effects options are in the Advanced tab of System Properties. Click Performance, Settings, then either pick 'Adjust for best performance' on the Visual Effects tab or turn individual effects on and off yourself.

Priorities

Still in the Performance Options dialog, go to the Advanced tab. Processor scheduling should always be set to Programs, but you can experiment with Memory usage. If you

have 128MB of RAM or less, set it to Programs; with 256MB or more, you might improve performance by putting more system information in memory. Set memory usage to System cache and reboot your machine.

Speed up serial

Windows XP defaults to a slow speed for your serial ports, which doesn't let your PC send information to your modem as fast as most modern computers could do. In Device Manager, open up the Ports (COM & LPT) tree and double click on each port in turn. On the Port Settings tab, change the Bits per second to the highest speed in the list and change Flow Control to hardware.

Turn off icons

Excessive desktop icons and desktop wallpaper take up their share of system memory. Animated desktops are particularly bad.

Faster browsing

If you're on a network, Windows XP scans all connected machines for scheduled tasks, slowing down your network speeds; stop it by deleting {D6277990-4C6A-11CF-8D87-00AA0060F5BF} from the HKEY_LOCAL_MACHINE\Software\Microsoft\Windows\CurrentVersion\Explorer\RemoteComputer\NameSpace\ key in the Registry, and Web pages will load faster.

Faster networks

Turn off Quality of Service (QoS) in Windows XP Professional to speed up networking by 20% – but don't turn it off in Networking Properties. Choose Start, Run and type 'gpedit.msc' to run the Local Group Policy Editor. Open Computer

Jargon

■ BIOS
The Basic Input/Output System is your PC's built-in software that lets your PC start up and control the keyboard, screen, disk drives, USB and serial ports and other built-in hardware.

■ IDE
Integrated Drive Electronics – a hard drive with a built-in controller, also known as Advanced Technology Attachment (ATA). Enhanced IDE extends IDE to larger hard drives with faster transfer speeds, and ATAPI lets you connect CD-ROM and DVD drives to the same controller as your hard drive.

■ DMA
The Basic Input/Output System is your PC's built-in software that lets your PC start up and control the keyboard, screen, disk drives, USB and serial ports and other built-in hardware.

Configuration, Administrative Templates, Network, QoS Packet Scheduler, Limit reservable bandwidth. Set this to Enabled, then take the Bandwidth limit from 20% down to 0.

Faster web access

In Internet Explorer, choose Tools, Internet Options, General and click Use Blank under Home Page. That way you don't have to wait for the home page to load when you start surfing.

Faster web access 2

Type a web address into the Start, Run box and you don't have to wait for the browser to open at all.

Prioritise programs

You can prioritise programs or services for processor time under System Properties, Advanced, Performance, Settings, Advanced, Processor Scheduling). Edit HKEY_LOCAL_MACHINE\System\CurrentControlSet\Control\PriorityControl\Win32PrioritySeparation in the Registry and you can fine tune this further. Try the max value of 38 (decimal) or experiment.

Prioritise programs

Run a demanding program with a higher priority: you can change the priority in Task Manager by right clicking on the process and choosing Set Priority; or you can use the START/HIGH command in the shortcut that runs the application.

Prioritise programs 2

Make a text file in Notepad with the text 'START/HIGH "%1" '. Save it as high.bat in your Windows directory, and make a shortcut to it in your Send To directory. Now you can right click on any program and use Send To, high.bat to run it with a high priority.

Shut down programs

If Windows XP takes ages to shut down programs that have crashed while it checks them, you can shorten the delay from the default 5 seconds by changing the Registry value HungAppTimeout value (in milliseconds) in the key HKEY_CURRENT_USER\Control Panel\Desktop.

Shut down Windows XP quickly

By default Windows XP gives programs 20 seconds to clean up after themselves when you shut down; you can shorten that time by changing the WaitToKillAppTimeout value (in milliseconds) in HKEY_CURRENT_USER\Control Panel\Desktop.

Shut down services quickly

Windows XP also waits for 20 seconds for each service to finish, so if your system takes a long time to shut down, try changing WaitToKillServiceTimeout in HKEY_LOCAL_MACHINE\SYSTEM\Current ControlSet\Control in the Registry.

Shut down programs automatically

Get Windows XP to automatically shut down applications when you shut Windows down: change the HKEY_CURRENT_USER\Control Panel\Desktop\AutoEndTasks key in the Registry to 1.

Analyse boot

Use the Bootvis tool to see what takes most time when your PC starts up, and to speed things up; choose Trace, Optimise System to have Bootvis speed up boot times or check if slow drivers or tasks are slowing you down. You can find Bootvis at http://download.microsoft.com/download/whistler/BTV/1.0/WXP/EN-US/BootVis-Tool.exe.

Optimise startup now

Windows XP collects information about how you use your applications, then rearranges your disk every three days to make it more efficient. You can force it to optimise straight away by running Bootvis, running the command line Disk Defragmenter (Start, Run, DEFRAG C: -B) or by choosing Start, Run and typing

RUNDLL32.EXE ADVAPI32.DLL, PROCESSIDLETASKS to optimise without doing an analysis or defrag.

Improve Prefetcher

The Prefetcher collects information about which files load when applications start, so Windows XP can have them ready to go: make it more efficient by changing EnablePrefetcher in the HKEY_LOCAL_MACHINE\SYSTEM\Current ControlSet\Control\Session Manager\ Memory Management\PrefetchParameters Registry key from 3 to 5.

Check startup

Type Start, Run, MSCONFIG and pick the Startup tab to see what programs start automatically when you run Windows XP: you'll often find programs you never use. Turn them off to start more quickly.

Turn off services

You may not need other background services so experiment with setting services to Manual so they can restart if needed. Help and Support takes a lot of resources but you need it to run the Help and Support Centre, so you'll have to make trade-offs between convenience and top performance.

To run a very demanding application or game, make a batch file to shut off all inessential services using the NET STOP command, and another to turn them back on afterwards with NET START.

Turn off indexing

Indexing makes searches faster by compiling files in the background, but you'll get better all-round performance by setting Indexing to manual. In the Performance and Maintenance Control Panel, choose Administrative Tools, Services. Now double click on Indexing service and click Stop. Finally, set Startup Type to Manual.

Trim fonts

If you've got more than 100 fonts installed, they'll take up a lot of resources – uninstall the ones you don't use.

Shortcuts to a faster PC

Access Windows XP system tools with simple keyboard shortcuts

A lot of these tips involve changing settings in the System Properties Control Panel. You can get at that by choosing the Performance and Maintenance Control Panel and clicking System, but it's quicker to press [Windows]+Pause Break to open it directly. The Windows XP Device Manager is on the Hardware tab. While the settings for System Restore are here too, the program itself is under Start, All Programs, Accessories, System Tools, along with Disk Cleaner and Disk Defragmenter.

Get at the Display Properties Control Panel quickly by right clicking on the desktop and choosing

Properties. You can launch the Task Manager by pressing Ctrl-Alt-Del or right clicking on the taskbar and choosing Task Manager. To run the Registry Editor, choose Start, Run and type REGEDIT. It's a good idea to make a backup of the Registry before you make any changes; you can do that by making a System Restore Point or by selecting the key you're going to change in the Registry Editor and choosing File, Export and saving the Selected Branch.

For other changes, you may need to edit the PC BIOS; when you switch your PC on, you'll see instructions for changing these settings.

Use NTFS

NTFS is a more efficient file system than FAT or FAT32: it's more reliable and doesn't need defragmenting as often.

Don't detect IDE

Windows XP checks the IDE controller for new drives every time you boot. If you use SCSI drives rather than IDE, turn off auto-detection in Device Manager to speed up booting. Open the IDE ATA/ATAPI Controllers and check the Advanced Settings for Primary and Secondary channels. Change Device Type from Auto Detection to None if you don't have a drive attached to that channel.

DMA

Are your hard drives transferring data at full speed? In Device Manager, right click on each drive channel; choose Properties, Advanced Settings. Transfer Mode should be set to DMA If it's available.

Ultra DMA

By default Windows XP doesn't support Ultra DMA 66; if your hard drive and controller use it, get faster data transfers by adding the DWORD value EnableUDMA66 (with a value of 1) under the Registry key HKEY_LOCAL_MACHINE\System\CurrentControlSet\Control\Class\{4D36E96A-E325-11CE-BFC1-08002BE10318}\0000\.

Disk caching

Write to disk more efficiently by doing it in bigger chunks. In Device Manager, open the Disk Drives tree, double click on your hard drive and choose Policies. Tick 'Enable write caching on the disk' and enable 'Optimize for performance'.

Digital audio

If you don't copy music tracks from CDs, turn off digital playback and speed your PC up. In Device Manager, open DVD/CD-ROM drives and double click on your drive; in the Properties tab, clear 'Enable digital CD audio'.

Defragment regularly

Although Windows XP optimises some files, run Disk Defragmenter once a fortnight to keep important files in one piece rather than in several fragments, so they load more quickly.

Third-party defrag

SpeedDisk (part of Norton Utilities) lets you put files that don't change at the end of the disk, where they won't get in the way of other files that do change size.

Fast video memory

Newer graphics cards and motherboards let you cache display data in video memory, so the card can write to screen in chunks rather than bit by bit. In your BIOS settings, look under Chip

Configuration for Video Memory Cache Mode and set it to USWC.

Remove old devices

If you remove a hard drive or a graphics card, Windows keeps the settings in the registry in case you put it back. In Device Manager, choose View, Show hidden devices and delete unused hardware.

Turn off ZIP

The built-in support for ZIP files uses a lot of resources: use a utility like WinZip instead and turn off ZIP support by choosing Start, Run and typing REGSVR32/U ZIPFLDR.DLL.

Unload DLLs

Windows XP keeps DLL files in memory after applications have finished using them. That can use lots of memory; try turning the cache off in the Registry by changing the value of HKEY_LOCAL_MACHINE\SOFTWARE\Micro soft\Windows\CurrentVersion\Explorer\Al waysUnloadDLL.

Automatic camera

Get Windows XP to automatically transfer pictures from your digital camera when you plug it in. Open My Computer and right click on the camera; choose Properties, Events, then pick the 'Save all pictures to this folder' button and choose a directory.

Single click

Get at everything with one less mouse click: in Explorer, choose Tools, Folder Options, 'Single click to open an item', and you won't need to double click.

See Control Panels

Add an icon for Control Panel to My Computer: go to Tools, Folder Options, View, Show Control panel in My Computer.

Make Control Panel a menu

Get at individual Control Panels directly. Right click on the Start menu; choose Properties, Start menu, Customise. Click set Control Panel to 'Display as a menu'.

Make Favourites a menu

Add your Internet Explorer Favourites to the Start menu: tick Favourites menu in the same Customize Start menu dialog to open Web pages faster. Do the same to My Documents, My Music, My Pictures, My Computer and Network Connections.

Reach recent

Still in the Customize dialog, tick 'List my most recently opened documents' to see recent images, text and HTML files.

Use Send To

Choose Start, Run and type SENDTO to open the Send To folder; create shortcuts to folders you use a lot, then move files quickly by right clicking; choose Send To.

Alphabetical menus

Internet Explorer favourites and other menus show up in the order you create them: right click and choose Sort by Name to make them alphabetical.

Favourite programs

The Start panel shows programs you've used recently: right click and choose Remove from List if you won't use them often. Drag them into the top half if you open them frequently.

Cache thumbnails

Get Windows XP to keep the thumbnails it generates for images in My Pictures. Choose Tools, Folder Options, View and clear 'Do not cache thumbnails'. ■

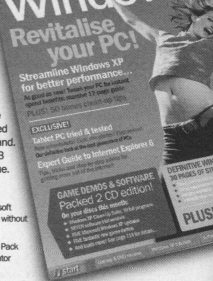

Why pay the full price for your copies of *Windows XP: The Official Magazine* when, by taking out a subscription, you'll get each copy for over £1 less than the cover price, plus free delivery?

Subscribing doesn't just save you money, though. It also guarantees that you won't miss an issue, so you'll be able to stay at the forefront of the latest Windows XP related developments, and take advantage of the fully working commercial programs we give away on our CD and DVD every issue.

You can subscribe by post, phone or at our website, and we offer a full money-back guarantee, meaning that you can cancel at any time and receive a refund on all unmailed issues.

Subscribe online

www.windowsxpmagazine.co.uk

Subscribe by phone

Hotline (UK only) **0870 444 8475**
Lines open 24 hours a day. Please quote code:
PCPXP01 when telephoning your order.
Overseas call **+44 1458 271100**
Overseas fax **+44 1225 822523**

Subscribe by post

Fill in the form and send to:
(UK) **Future Publishing, FREEPOST BS4900, Somerton, Somerset, TA11 6BR**
(Overseas) **Future Publishing, Cary Court, Somerton, Somerset, TA11 6TB, UK**

YES! I WANT 13 ISSUES OF WINDOWS XP: THE OFFICIAL MAGAZINE

Type of subscription	CD version	DVD version
UK Direct Debit	☐ £64.84	☐ £69.96
UK Credit Card	☐ £64.84	☐ £69.96
US/Europe	☐ £89.94	☐ £94.94
Rest of World	☐ £94.99	☐ £99.99

PAYEE'S DETAILS

Title ....Initials ....
Surname.................
Address ....
....Postcode ....
Country.................Tel no. (inc. STD) ....
Email address...

Your subscription will start with the next available issue

METHOD OF PAYMENT I understand that I will receive 13 issues

☐ Direct Debit – CD (UK only) I would like to pay £16.21 every 3 months.
☐ Direct Debit – DVD (UK only) I would like to pay £17.49 every 3 months.
☐ Cheque (£ sterling drawn on a UK bank account payable to Future Publishing Ltd)
☐ Switch ☐ Mastercard ☐ Visa ☐ American Express

Card no.

☐☐☐☐ ☐☐☐☐☐☐ ☐☐☐☐

Expiry date ☐☐ ☐☐

Switch only: issue no. ☐☐☐☐ valid date ☐☐ ☐☐

Signature _____ Date _____

☐ Please tick here if you do not wish to receive mail from Future Publishing and other carefully selected companies

Send to: Windows XP: The Official Magazine, Subscriptions
UK: Future Publishing, **FREEPOST BS4900**, Somerton, Somerset, TA11 6BR.
Overseas: Future Publishing, Cary Court, Somerton, Somerset TA11 6TB, UK.

Instruction to your Bank or Building Society to pay Direct Debits.

future publishing
Media with passion

DIRECT Debit

Originator's Identification Number
7 6 8 1 9 5

Future Publishing Ltd. Cary Court, Somerton, Somerset, TA11 6BR

1. Name and full postal address of your Bank or Building Society branch
To: The Manager_____Bank/Building Society
Address _____
_____
_____Postcode_____

2. Name(s) of account holder(s)

3. Branch sort code
(from the top right hand corner of your cheque) ☐☐ ☐☐ ☐☐

4. Bank or Building Society account number ☐☐☐☐☐☐☐☐

5. Instruction to your Bank or Building Society
Please pay Future Publishing Direct Debits from the account detailed on this Instruction subject to the safeguards assured by the Direct Debit Guarantee. I understand that this Instruction may remain with Future Publishing and if so, details will be passed electronically to my bank or building society.

Signature(s)_____Date_____

Ref No (Office use only)_____
Banks and Building Societies may not accept Direct Debit Instructions for some types of account.

ORDER CODE: **PCPXP01**

Credits

EDITORIAL IS AT
30 Monmouth Street, Bath, BA1 2BW
Tel 01225 442244 **Fax** 01225 462986

Editor **David Bradley** xp.editor@futurenet.co.uk
Senior Art Editor **Dylan Channon** dylan.channon@futurenet.co.uk

BOOK COMPILATION AND DESIGN
Steve Croucher, Steve Farragher, Sarah Williams

Production co-ordinator **Lee Thomas** lee.thomas@futurenet.co.uk

Managing Editor **Nick Merritt** nick.merritt@futurenet.co.uk
Group Art Editor **Paul McIntyre** paul.mcintyre@futurenet.co.uk
Publisher **Dave Taylor** dave.taylor@futurenet.co.uk
Publishing Director **John Weir** john.weir@futurenet.co.uk

Future Publishing Ltd. is part of the Future Network plc.
We aim to offer superb value for money, trustworthy information,
multiple ways to save time and money, and mags that are a pleasure to read or visit.
The Future Network plc is a public company quoted
on the London Stock Exchange (symbol: FNET).

Chief Executive **Greg Ingham**
Managing Director **Colin Morrison**
www.thefuturenetwork.plc.uk

Printed in the UK.
■ All content © 2002 Future Publishing Ltd.

Produced in association with

Microsoft (UK)